Machine Learning for Beginners

The Ultimate Guide to Learn and Understand Machine Learning – A Practical Approach to Master Machine Learning to Improve and Increase Business Results

Anderson Coen

© **Copyright 2019 - Anderson Coen - All rights reserved.**

The content contained within this book may not be reproduced, duplicated or transmitted without direct written permission from the author or the publisher.

Under no circumstances will any blame or legal responsibility be held against the publisher, or author, for any damages, reparation, or monetary loss due to the information contained within this book, either directly or indirectly.

Legal Notice:

This book is copyright protected. It is only for personal use. You cannot amend, distribute, sell, use, quote or paraphrase any part, or the content within this book, without the consent of the author or publisher.

Disclaimer Notice:

Please note the information contained within this document is for educational and entertainment purposes only. All effort has been executed to present accurate, up to date, reliable, complete information. No warranties of any kind are declared or implied. Readers acknowledge that the author is not engaging in the rendering of legal, financial, medical or professional advice. The content within this book has been derived from various sources. Please consult a licensed professional before attempting any techniques outlined in this book.

Description

By reading this document, the reader agrees that under no circumstances is the author responsible for any losses, direct or indirect, that are incurred as a result of the use of information contained within this document, including, but not limited to, errors, omissions, or inaccuracies.

What is machine learning? Does it really help businesses provide better services and earn more? How can I improve my business processes to increase ROI (Return On Investment)? I am unable to focus on important tasks because I am getting bogged down by menial tasks. If you are confronted by one or more of these questions, this book is for you!

You should also get this book if you have heard machine learning but couldn't start because it looks too overwhelming. This book will demonstrate it's quite easy, and many situations have similar solutions – the only things needed are a bit of conceptual knowledge and some free time.

Learn machine learning and data analysis concepts through practical examples coded in Python. The following libraries are covered in great detail:

- NumPy
- SciPy
- Sklearn (Scikit-learn)
- Pandas

- TensorFlow
- Matplotlib

There's also a chapter dedicated for an introduction to Raspberry Pi. If you are interested in robotics and automation, this chapter is not to be missed. Machine learning is being used in industries that are not directly related to computer science. If you are new to Python, there is also an introductory chapter that covers the basics, so you can start with data analysis and machine learning as soon as possible. Buy this book and start your machine learning journey today!

Table of Contents

Introduction 1

Chapter 1: Machine Learning 5

    What Is Machine Learning Really? 6

        Types of Machine Learning 10

        More Categories of Machine Learning 14

        Machine-Learning Challenges 16

        Present Day Examples 20

Chapter 2: Coding with Python 23

    Fundamental Programming 24

        Setup 25

        Initializing PyCharm 29

        Data Structures 37

        Advanced Programming 56

    Revisiting Mathematical Concepts 66

        Vectors 66

        Matrices 71

        Basic Statistics 74

        Probability 79

        Distribution 81

    Data Analysis – Foundation of Machine Learning 83

        Python Libraries for Data Analysis 83

        The Pandas Framework 132

    Machine-Learning Projects 164

 Predicting If a Country's GDP is Related to Its Better Life Index 164

 Predicting Real Estate Prices for Investment 166

Chapter 3: Working with Raspberry Pi 183

 What is Raspberry Pi? 183

  Selecting the Model 184

  Hardware Components 185

 First Project 186

  Installation and Setup 186

  Remote Access to Raspberry Pi 190

  Using Camera with Raspberry Pi 193

  Sending and Receiving Signals Using GPIO of the Raspberry Pi 197

Chapter 4: Working with TensorFlow 208

 The Projects 208

  Project #1: Predicting Student Grade 209

  Project #2: Predicting Student Grade 212

  Project #3: Neural Network using TensorFlow 229

Chapter 5: Advanced Machine Learning 234

 A Corporate Project 234

  Create a Predictive Chat Bot 234

Conclusion 242

 Where Will Machine Learning Be in the Next 20 Years? 242

References 244

Appendix A: Machine-Learning Concepts 245

Introduction

Flying without wings, breathing underwater without gills, climbing mountains, inventing cures for incurable diseases, taming elemental powers, landing on the moon, the list of human feats is never-ending. But, there is one thing that has always eluded mankind – predicting the future. The biggest disadvantage humans have is never knowing when they are going to die. There is no way to predict future events with certainty. With all the technological advancements, the biggest questions are still unanswered. Will human beings ever be able to correctly predict the future?

Let me ask you a question. Did anyone in the past come close to predicting the future? How can you know without access to relevant information? The relevant information required to make a decision is generated from analyzing accumulated in the past is called data analysis. If we take the same process a little further, create trends from existing data and use them to predict future outcomes, we enter the domain called data science.

And, it's not just about making decisions; for humans, it's a matter of survival and growth. Every child relies heavily on data analysis to perform experiments, gather environment responses, and analyze them to learn and adapt. When a mother scolds her child because he threw the bowl across the room, he learns to not do that again. When the same mother hugs and kisses the child when the first word they say is "ma," the child learns that to speak this word is happiness, and will always feel happy saying it for the rest of his life.

So, where does machine learning fits on all this? Machines are great at doing repetitive tasks, but a programmer has to write a script to tackle every possible scenario for the machine to work efficiently. What if, just like a child, the machine could learn from their experiences and experiments? Instead of telling the machine what to do for all possible situations, the machine is told a set of rules. In case an unfamiliar situation happens, the machine will determine the appropriate response using the rules and gauge the environment response. If it was favorable, the machine will record it and apply the same response in a similar situation later on. If an unfavorable response is met, the machine will use the set of rules again and start over if a similar situation happens again.

We know that real-life scenarios are much more complex than machine logics. Applying the same logic on similar situations isn't suitable when dealing with complex variables, such as humans. Consider a robot, Ms. X, who is the maid of a household. The first time she meets her charge, she tries to joke in front of the little Jana, and she bursts into laughter. Ms. X recorded this as a successful experiment and during dinner the same night and cracked the same joke. Jana's older brother Jack commented, "That's the lamest joke ever." Ms. X is now confused. A human being wouldn't be confused in these circumstances; it knows a joke might be funny to one person but not for someone else. You might think this is just basic, but in fact, learning this intricacy is one of the things that sets humans at the top of the animal kingdom.

You might have seen a sci-fi movie or read a futuristic novel that talks about a hive mind. A collection of robots or machines that have come together to unlock unlimited processing power gaining abilities like future prediction, imminent threat detection, then eventually conquering and controlling the human race. Well, it might be or not be true in the future; one thing is for certain, we are moving towards fully enlightened independent robots that can thrive on their own.

The project of machine learning has one main goal – to give machines the degree of learning and inference capabilities humans possess. Maybe when machines reach that level, they would be able to accurately predict the demise of humans and this planet.

I assume you have some basic knowledge about computers and programming languages before you started reading this book. Don't worry, every topic I cover in this book, I will explain right from the basics. I am also assuming you have access to a good, stable internet connection and an upgraded computer system in good condition. Data analysis and machine learning algorithms put a lot of strain on the computer resources. My Master's degree thesis was to improve an already well-optimized algorithm. The data set was huge and the algorithm was very complex. I didn't have access to a computer with a powerful configuration. I still remember how I had to leave the computer on for 20-22 hours for the program to finish processing. If you want to learn machine learning, start saving, and invest in the latest computer system.

Chapter 1: Machine Learning

Watch the Terminator movie series if you haven't. It indirectly portrays robots following the age old saying, *"If at first you don't succeed, try, try again!"* The machine network, SkyNet, created by scientists to facilitate humans in research and development, gets affected by illusions of grandeur. Assuming machines are the dominant race, SkyNet attacks humans. One thing leads to another and SkyNet has to send robots to the past to neutralize one human threat that was the cause of Skynet's destruction in the future.

SkyNet sends one robot, who, after a lot of trouble and the hero getting killed in the process, gets sent to the scrapyard by the heroine. SkyNet learns from the encounter and the next time sends an upgraded robot. Yes, machine learning at its finest! Well, without recalling anything else from the movie franchise, here's the moral of the entire series: machines are faster at processing in a given direction but humans are faster at adapting in fluid situations. No matter what kind of robot SkyNet threw out of the production facility, the human protagonists, albeit taking heavy losses and many times aided by some machines, always adapted and defeated the *evil* machines. The first installment of this movie franchise was released in 1980s starring Arnold Schwarzenegger as the time travelling robot. It was an instant hit.

But, why I am talking about a movie franchise in a book about machine learning? The general public in the 1980s had no idea about fully automated robots. In 2019, it looks very likely we are going to see fully automated robots in two or three decades. Many things that are now part of everyone's lives or look very much possible in the near future have been inspired by movies. Movie and television franchises like Star Wars and Star Trek have influenced scientific development for decades. Therefore, it's important not to ignore this avenue of inspirations.

Do you remember a movie or TV show where the plot revolves around machine learning?

What Is Machine Learning Really?

Often considered a part of Artificial Intelligence (AI), machine learning is described as the reliance of a machine on pattern detection and situational inference instead of a predetermined set of instructions and the scientific study of statistical models and algorithms that enable machines to achieve instructional independence.

Artificial Intelligence, you might be thinking, why I didn't say that before? Now, that's a phrase you would have heard in many movies and TV shows. Sci-fi movies based on deep space exploration have spaceships operated by AI that enables the human crew to hibernate in special pods for decades. But, as is the twist in almost every one of them, the crew is forcibly awakened due to a catastrophic accident the ship has experienced due to a problem in AI.

But what does it mean that machine learning is a part of AI? For anything to be considered intelligent, it must have several qualities, and learning-on-the-go is just one of them. It means a machine might not have AI even though it learns from the collected data.

The human mind is the most complex and brilliant machine in the known world. What makes the human mind the best machine in the world up till now? The ability to relate complex situations and infer a possible course-of-action. The human mind can imagine and discuss abstract matters. In case of immediate danger to the human, the mind can shut off all non-essential systems to prioritize survival protocols. An organic machine that can arguably operate at the speed of light? That's definitely a marvel.

But, the human mind is limited by the body that holds it. The best analogy for the human mind and body is attaching a lightspeed engine to a tortoise; the potential is infinite but limited by the host's physical characteristics. This leads to the answers of a question everything thinks about when starting to learn machine learning.

"Why are we trying to give machines the ability to learn and make decisions on their own?" I thought about this question a

lot, and I assume, before moving forward, you would also like to know the answer to this question. The blunt answer is, humans are lazy with limited physical strength.

1. Humans don't like performing repetitive tasks, it gets boring fast.
2. An average human can't lift more than its body weight.
3. Humans are slow with numbers and symbols in general.
4. Humans require frequent breaks.
5. The performance of a human being is directly proportional to its mood or mental health.
6. An average human being has a running speed of 45 km/h and no human can sustain that speed for long.
7. Humans require a very specific thriving environment just to survive.

To overcome all these challenges, humans invented machines. From a wheel to a crane, spaceships to submarines, humans have developed machines for every imaginable challenge possible. This is an amazing feat, but also highlights a serious problem. Humans have to develop a machine specific to each challenge or modify it to meet the requirements of another challenge. The Challenger 2 tank can't do what a Lamborghini can do, a Typhoon can't do what Saturn V can do. You might say, I am comparing apples to oranges; okay, another example, can you drive a Jetta and Lamborghini? Here are a few of the reasons why the world is looking towards machine learning.

1. Creating a new machine every time a new feature is required is financially expensive and a huge strain on resources. Remember the classical typewriter? How difficult it was to type and maintain the machine, how difficult it was to add erasing capabilities to the typewriter? A digital keyboard not only made the typing and corrections faster but, also, reduced maintenance costs in the long run.

2. If the input data is very large in size, it is difficult to find a connection without the help of a machine. Consider a police officer who has to manually go through thousands of records to match the photo of a suspect captured by a security camera. With image processing and machine learning, a software will be able to search the records for the right person, even if you have a side pose of the suspect in the captured image.

3. How many times does a designed prototype ace the test but fails on the very first day of real-world application? Back it goes to the testing facility, wasting some more

millions of taxpayer dollars on experiments. It usually happens because the prototype designers failed to consider a specific real-world scenario during the design and testing. What if the machine had the capacity to modify itself in unexpected conditions? It would save millions of dollars in prototyping and experimentation stages.

Types of Machine Learning

There are three broad types of machine learning:

1. Supervised learning
2. Unsupervised learning
3. Reinforcement learning

Supervised Learning

A type of machine learning where the machine learns the system by training on a set of sample data that lead to the desired output. Once the machine is ready, live data is fed, and the machine predicts future outcomes using the relation it has established during the training. Supervised learning is a popular type of machine learning in beginners. Most people starting with machine learning find supervised learning easier to understand. Why wouldn't they? This is how humans learn too!

Classification

An example would be an email filtering system that sends and directs emails sent to you to either your inbox or spam folder. This type of supervised learning is called classification where labels are given to data. The system will be trained on existing emails that have been correctly directed, so the system can build a relation and automatically direct emails in the future. A system that classifies data into two classes (spam or inbox in this case) is called a binary classification system.

If you have the Outlook.com email service from Microsoft, you might have noticed, there's no way to set a spam filter that most email services provide. Instead, you have to manually move emails from inbox to spam folder and vice versa. The email filter of Outlook.com learns by monitoring your actions, and with time, the spam filtering becomes smarter. It might feel like a hassle in the start, but it becomes very convenient on the long-term as you don't have to worry about blocking every single email address or every keyword in the spam filter. Of course, in a complex system like Outlook.com, labeling an email as spam or not is not the only classification task. All such systems that have various classifications are called multi-class classification system. A better example of a multi-class classification is gesture recognition now widely available in smartphones. During setup, the smartphone trains on user gestures to recognize and differentiate personalized versions of gestures.

<u>Regression</u>

The machine learning applied to systems that take some inputs and produce continuous outputs is called regression analysis. The system is defined by a number of (explanatory) variables that are considered to affect the system in a way that it continuously produces a response variable (outcome). The analysis finds the relation between the explanatory and outcome variables to predict future system behavior.

A real-life example would to predict the SAT scores of a few students by sampling their life and study patterns. Using the data gathered from students who have already given the test as training for the prediction model, the learning model will have the ability to predict which future students will have more chances of passing the test using their behavioral data.

Reinforcement Learning

In reinforcement learning, there is a sort of feedback mechanism (or function) that provides reward signals when the machine-learning model interacts with a given system. The signals are used to gradually improve the learning model. We can say this is the automated trial-and-error method of machine learning. Reinforcement learning differs from the supervised learning in the sense that in the former learning model, the machine directly interacts with the system rather than using previous user-system interactions to learn and predict future outcomes.

The perfect example of reinforcement learning would be a strategy game where the computer learns the moves made by the player and gradually learns to finally beat every move of the player.

Unsupervised Learning

In both supervised and reinforcement machine learning analysis, we would already know the system's response to a given set of inputs either by sampling previous interactions or having the machine interact with the system. But, what if we have to deal with a data set without knowing what outcome it results in or what feedback it gives when applied to a system? We have to resort to unsupervised learning analysis, where meaningful information is extracted from a data set without knowing the outcome or feedback of the system. In other words, the data is analyzed without considering any of the system's attributes to predict future behavior of the system.

Clustering

A technique of categorizing data into subgroups (clusters) without any prior knowledge of the data is called clustering. For example, online marketers would like to segment the audience based upon their interests without knowing how they would interact or have interacted with their marketing campaign. This helps marketers to predict the audience response and create targeted marketing campaigns for different audience segments.

Another practical application of clustering would be to find anomalies in a system. For example, a bank would deploy a learning model that tracks all credit card transactions of a client creating a spending profile. Using this profile, the system would be able to detect outlier transactions that might be a case of theft or fraud.

More Categories of Machine Learning

We can also categorize machine learning systems on their ability to generalize. In simpler terms, when predicting an action or decision for a future event, it should be able to generalize that event as the same or similar to an event it encountered during training. Performing well during the training doesn't equate to performing well during live action.

So, how do machine learning systems generalize? There are two approaches to this.

Instance-based

The easiest way of learning something is to *learn by heart*. But, this approach becomes tedious over time because memory is limited (in case of machines) and flawed (in the case of humans). A better way is to perform generalization to reach a new conclusion. For example, you know that you need 5 minutes to walk from your house to the corner store. Now, if you want to visit Ben who lives just across the corner store, you would generalize that you would need roughly 5 to 6 minutes to reach his house (the extra minute to cross the road). Let's take the example of the email filtering system that learns by tracking your actions of marking different emails as spam. The first phase would be to *learn by heart* and mark all identical emails as spam. The next phase would be to find a measure of similarity between the emails marked as spam and automatically generalize future emails according to that similarity model. The measure of similarity can be anything, such as specific words in the subject or specific email domains, even the time of reception can be used to find similarity. This will not be a 100% accurate filtering system, but makes things much easier for the end-user.

Model-based

Another way of generalization is to create a model for the system during training and use that model for predicting future events and outcomes. For example, we would like to know if there's any relation between money and happiness in people's lives. We gather the required data and plot it to see if there's any trend. If there's a visible trend, albeit with a few outliers, we can devise a model according to the trend. If the trend is linear, we can start with a simpler linear model. Here's an example.

happiness = $\theta_0 + \theta_1 \times$ money

The $\theta_0 + \theta_1$ are two linear model parameters that we need to find value for before we can start using this model for prediction. To find the values of these parameters, we can test the performance of our model by either using a utility function that tells how good our model is, or a cost function that tells how bad our model is. For linear models, the cost function makes more sense as we can determine how far the model predictions are from the training data. Using a linear-regression algorithm for training, the gap is minimized that results in the best possible values for the model parameters.

Once the model parameters are decided, we can use it for predictions. In a later chapter, we are going to take a look at the Python script to create a linear model to find if money and happiness are truly related.

Sometimes your model will not make good predictions. In that case, you might want to include more data attributes to the model or use a better model (such as polynomial-regression model instead of the linear one).

Machine-Learning Challenges

Machine learning is heavily dependent on the training data and the model (and algorithm) chosen to represent the system. Let's see what can happen that fails your machine-learning project.

Insufficient Training Data

Humans can work with very small data set and reach the correct conclusions. You touch a hot iron and you will probably be cautious around an iron for the rest of your lives. You might see dark clouds and a fearful storm once in your life and whenever you see those same clouds again, you will know a storm is coming. This process starts right from the childbirth and keeps going until the death. Machines are not so smart, you might say. They require considerable data to train a machine in using a particular prediction algorithm. For example, for a successful image recognition project, you might need access to millions of images as training data.

Various researches in the last two decades have found the same conclusion: instead of spending resources on better algorithms, spend resources on collection of large data sets because, given the right amount of data, many algorithms will reach the same conclusion.

Similar but Not the Same Training Data

For example, you write a script to predict traffic congestion on major New York highways during rush hours but train it using data collected from Los Angeles. The data might be of similar type but has no relation with the scenario we will use our script to predict. We have to make sure the training data represents the right scenarios.

Poor Quality or Skewed Data

The training data must be free of or contain minimal errors, noise, and/or outliers. Training a model using erroneous data will affect its performance in making the right predictions. A better approach would be to clean the training data, and in fact, most data scientists spend more time preparing the training data than coding the model and algorithm. Important considerations must be need in how to deal with outliers (discard or normalize) and missing data (ignore or fill in with values such as mean, etc.).

Another aspect of sampling training data is to make sure the data isn't skewed or biased. For example, how many times you have seen poll results and accompanied predictions that you know are completely wrong. The most obvious reason is that the participants of the poll aren't representative of the whole situation. For example, if 1,000 US residents from Idaho took part in a poll, you can't use this data to make predictions for the entire USA.

Say No to Overfitting

Humans tend to blow up the extent of their experience and apply indiscriminately. How many times the restaurant waiter or manager has come to your table and ask for your feedback and you have replied, "Everything was amazing!" even though the fries weren't good. Consider there are 100 people who order fries every day from the restaurant, the waiters and manager are able to collect feedback from 60 people and only 5% of those told them the fries are bad. The restaurant would discard those three reviews thinking they are outliers even though they are indicative of a serious issue. This is how overgeneralization can truly ruin a successful business.

Another example would be you going on a tourist vacation to a foreign country. The taxi driver you hired from the airport to your hotel charges steep rates. Due to the frustrating experience, you might form the opinion that all taxi drivers in that country are manipulators, and you might even avoid taking a taxi for the rest of your trip. Of course, this is a case of overgeneralized opinion that doesn't portray thc facts.

Machines can also fall into the same pit; in machine learning it's called overfitting. Overfitted data can be a serious issue because the model will perform exceptionally well on such data during training but fail miserably when given live data. The process of reducing such overfitting risks is called regularization.

Underfitting Is Trouble Too

Underfitting is the opposite of underfitting and is caused by the model not able to properly detect the subtleness of training data. Relating money with happiness is an issue that's too complex to accurately predict; there are infinite variables that can affect the relationship. Therefore, a model to predict this behavior will never be 100% accurate because it cannot accommodate all those variables.

Bonus: Testing

How do you test a prediction model after training? You wouldn't want to ship it to the users for testing because if they have paid for the product, and the prediction results are coming up as wrong, your business will suffer. In some industries, this is the norm; for example, gaming studios release alpha and beta versions that are free to play and test and then predict performance once the game is available for purchase. But in other industries, it's important to test before releasing the product to the public. One of the basic procedures to perform testing is to divide the training data into two parts, a training set and a test set. This way, you don't need to worry about testing data after you have trained your model using the training set.

Present Day Examples

Machine learning is still rapidly evolving, but it has become vital in many industries. Machine learning is helping professionals in various fields to reach new conclusions that were impossible before. Here are a few examples.

Image Recognition

The modern age is all about images and videos. With the boom of social media, the selfie craze and the hugely improved smartphone cameras, everyone captures an image every day. Have you ever uploaded photos on Facebook and saw the people in them get automatically tagged? Smartphones have now facial locks so you can lock/unlock your phone using you face. There are applications that converts handwriting into typed words by learning the user's hand strokes.

Speech Recognition

We are very close to getting fully smart homes that you will be able to control just by using your voice. There are already services like Alexa that recognize voice commands and perform the actions. Depending upon the make of your smartphone, there is a virtual assistant that you can activate to give voice commands. There is also high-level dictation software used by professionals that learn the characteristics of the user's voice and offer high speed speech to text service.

Medical Applications

Machine learning has enabled medical professionals to find new cures and predict viral outbreaks. By analyzing tracked information of the patients, accurate predictions can be made remotely in regards to health deterioration and onset of illness. Applying the image recognition benefits of machine learning with medical imaging techniques such as MRI, etc., helps detect diseases at a nascent age that a doctor's naked eye might miss.

Finance and Trading

Machine learning can also help with stock trading and making better financial decisions through accurate market predictions. Various algorithm techniques are used to find correlation between different signals and used to formulate a short-term investment strategy.

Product Associations

It is very important for businesses to find the impact of one product over the other. For example, McDonalds might want to predict what impact discontinuing an item would have on the sales of other items before making the decision.

Classification

Government and private institutions like to classify people and clients according to their risk potential. For example, your bank would like to use your financial history to predict your future before accepting your loan application.

Customer Sentiment

Businesses would like the predict customer sentiment before launching a new brand. This is extremely useful to choose the correct time for launch to maximize customer participation. This might include competitor analysis and case studies of similar businesses.

Artificial Intelligence

Machine learning is considered a stepping stone in achieving complete artificial intelligence. Consider a system that's fully aware of all its parameters and already knows the future outcomes if any of those parameters change. It would require tremendous processing power but will help humans achieve unimaginable results. There are governments already considering the use robots to avoid losing precious human lives in wars. How about sending robot in space that have the same mind power of a human but aren't constrained by the physical attributes of human body? We might be able to mine different planets of the solar system for resources that are already running out on Earth.

Chapter 2: Coding with Python

Python is a multi-purpose language. It means it can be used to code and resolve issues in various applications. Starting out as a *simple to write, simple to read* programming language, it has grown into the most popular language in the data analysis and machine-learning industries.

But, why did Python become so popular in data analysis compared to languages with similar capabilities? Data analysis can be used in any field, including finance and medical. People who are not professional programmers have to *crunch* numbers for analysis and research. A programming language that's easier to code but powerful enough to handle complex data generated in real-life applications was bound to become popular.

The open-source nature of the programming language also helped spread its use because many online and offline instructors adopted Python to teach various algorithms and programming techniques. When you are new, there is usually a lot of confusion and you need as much resources as you can find.

Due to numerous, highly varied applications of the programming language, organizations and volunteers have published different packages (usually called distributions) to facilitate faster and easier startup. If you want to learn the basics of programming and Python, you can start with using any online Python environment. One such example is https://repl.it/languages/python3

Fundamental Programming

For this book, I have chosen to use PyCharm and Anaconda with Python 3.7. PyCharm is a very popular and sophisticated Integrated Development Environment (IDE) that provides various advantages over IDLE, the standard Python IDE. Anaconda is a specialized distribution that provides all the libraries related to data analysis and machine learning by default. It helps programmers avoid wasting time on finding and installing the required libraries that don't come with the standard Python distribution.

Anaconda also provides a package management system "conda" that helps create virtual environments. Virtual environments are used to install different setups for different projects on the same computer system. It helps avoid conflicts between packages. If you are going to only work on one application for the rest of your life (which is rarely the case), you can skip virtual environment setup. But, it's highly recommended.

Setup

Setting up PyCharm and Anaconda is a bit tricky, so make sure you go through the process with utmost care. One small mistake can break the connection between PyCharm and Anaconda.

Install PyCharm

Go to the website URL https://www.jetbrains.com/pycharm/download/ to download the latest version of PyCharm for your system. The link will automatically redirect to the correct URL for your operation system, for example, for me running Windows, the URL becomes https://www.jetbrains.com/pycharm/download/#section=windows.

Select the "community" version, so you don't have to pay in the future. After the download is complete, start the installation process. Make sure to check the "Add launchers dir to the PATH" option, in the window below.

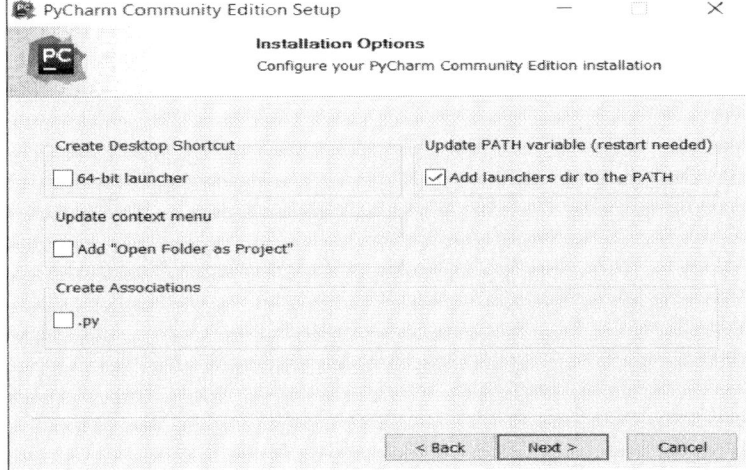

I installed PyCharm in the same directory where Python is installed but that's optional.

Install Anaconda

Go to the URL https://www.anaconda.com/distribution/, download the correct installer (I chose the one for Windows – 64 bit), and install once the download is complete. Note that Anaconda is a huge distribution without hundreds, if not thousands, of Python libraries. After-install size is a staggering figure of 2.5 Gigabytes (GB). During the install, you will see the following screen; make sure you check the box that says "Add Anaconda to my PATH environment variable" even though it isn't advised. Checking this option will make your life a lot easier using Anaconda in the future.

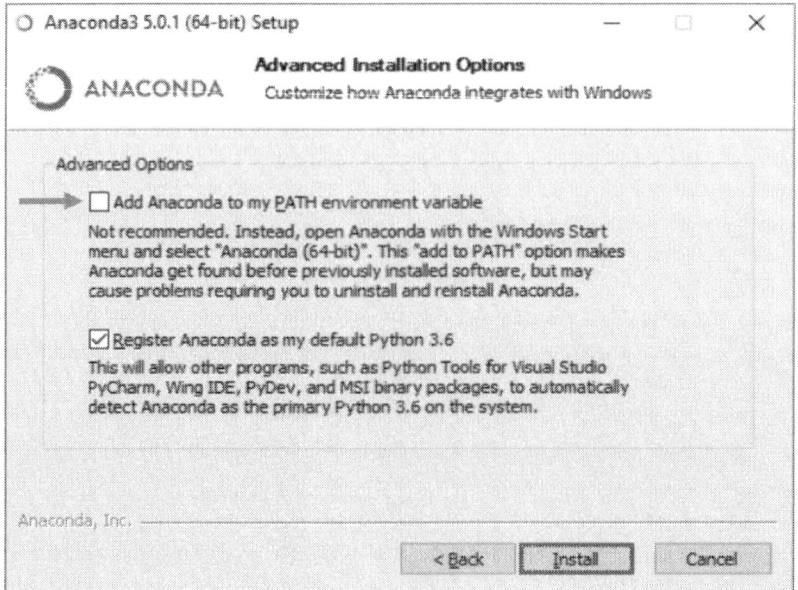

The installation can take a considerable amount of time depending upon the computational power of your computer system. After the installation is done, we can test if Anaconda is working correctly. Open Windows start menu and type "Anaconda Prompt". Type "python" and Python will start.

Bonus: Install TensorFlow

TensorFlow is a great platform to build and train machine-learning models. Let's install it on our system using a virtual environment. What was a virtual environment? To create isolated spaces to keep required tools, libraries, etc., separate for different projects, virtual environments are used. This is very useful for programming languages that can be used for multiple application fields. Imagine yourself working on two projects, one on machine learning and one on developing a 2D game. Creating a virtual environment would help keep things organized for both projects.

Let's open Windows command prompt. We are going to use Anaconda to create a virtual environment and install TensorFlow in it. The latest version of TensorFlow 2.0 is still not fully compatible with standard Python 3.7. You can find so many programmers running into issues trying to install TensorFlow 2.0 on Python 3.7. This is another reason to use Anaconda to install TensorFlow; you will avoid any compatibility issues. Enter the following command in the Windows command prompt to create a virtual environment and install the platform in it.

```
conda create -n tf TensorFlow
```

"-n" means new, "tf" is the name we gave to the virtual environment getting created with "TensorFlow" installed in it. During the install, you might be asked to proceed with installing some new packages. Just type "y" and hit "ENTER" to continue. Once complete, you can activate this newly created virtual environment with the following command.

```
conda activate tf
```

You will now see "(tf)" written before the current path in the command prompt. It tells you are working in a virtual environment.

Bonus: Install Keras

Keras is a high-level API for creating neural networks using Python. While we are in the same virtual environment "tf," we can invoke the standard Python package manager "pip" to install Keras.

```
pip install keras
```

Once everything is installed and ready, we can jump to PyCharm to finalize the setup and starting coding.

Initializing PyCharm

Search "pycharm" in Windows start menu and you will see an option that says "JetBrains PyCharm Community Edition...". Select the option and wait for a window to pop up. This is how it would look like.

Click on "Create New Project" to start. It will ask for a location and name. I used "tensorEnv" as project name; you can choose whatever name you like.

Now, the PyCharm interface will load. Right-click where it says "tensorEnv" in the "Project" and select "New" and then "Python File". Enter a name; I used "test.py".

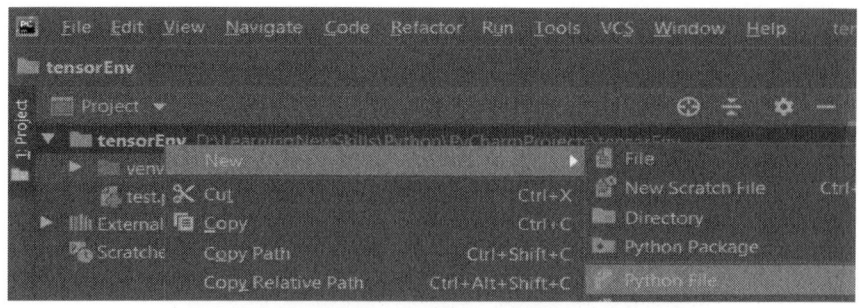

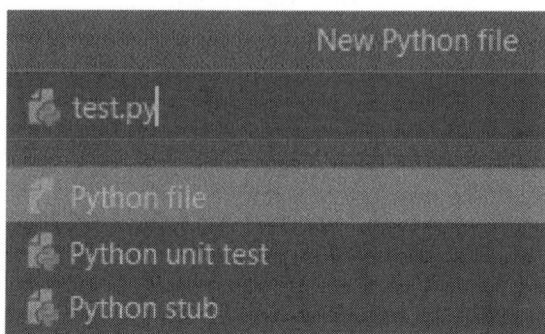

There's two more steps to do. First is setting the right Python interpreter for the project and then adding a configuration to the project. Click on "File", and select "Settings". In the new pop up, select "Project Interpreter" under "Project: tensorEnv".

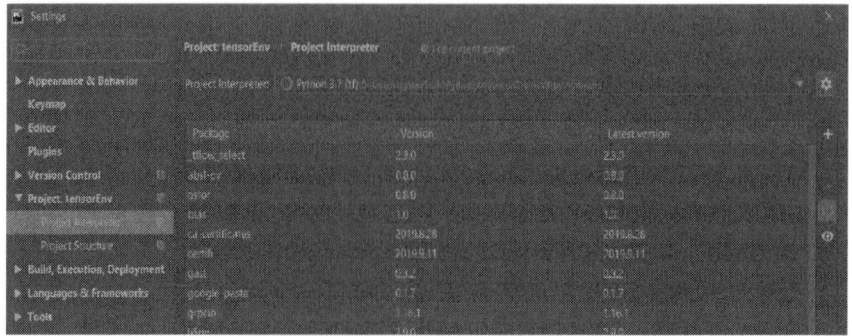

Click on the gear icon on the right side of the screen, select "Add..." You will see a new window on your screen.

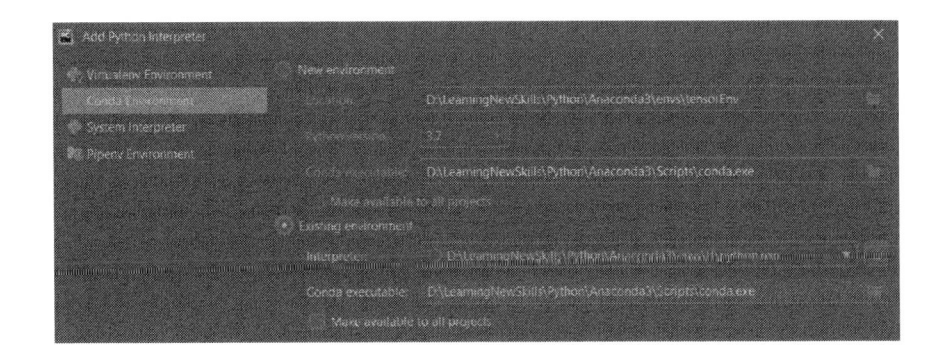

Select "Conda Environment" and then select "Existing environment". In the above image, you are seeing the following value in the "Interpreter" field.

D:\LearningNewSkills\Python\Anaconda3\envs\tf\python.exe

For you, that field might be empty. We have to navigate and select the correct interpreter "pythonw.exe" for our project (notice the 'w'). Hint: "python.exe" and "pythonw.exe" are usually in the same folder. Remember "tf" in the above path is the environment we created using Windows command prompt. Replace "tf" with the environment name you used then when looking for the right folder. Once the right file is selected, click "OK" until you are back on the main PyCharm interface.

Now, we have to setup the configuration. Click on "Add Configuration" on the top-right side of the screen.

Click on the '+' sign and then select "Python".

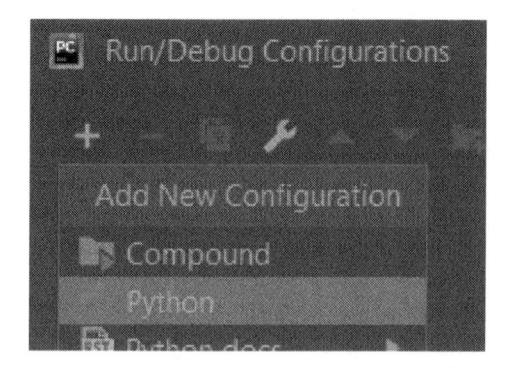

In the new window, add the name you want for the configuration. Usually, the name should be the same as the file you created before, so we are going to use "test". In the "Script path" field, click on the folder icon and navigate to the file you created, which is "test.py" in our case. Once the file is selected, click "OK" until you are back on the main PyCharm interface.

If you are thinking this is quite complex, you are right. Good news is, you don't need to do all the steps every time you start a new project. You also don't need to use PyCharm, which is just the IDE. You can install Anaconda, TensorFlow, and Keras on the standard IDLE. But, PyCharm is worth all the trouble we just went through.

Let's do the "Hello, World" program. In the test.py we created, write the following line of code.

print('Hello, World!')

To run the script, click on "Run" and then "Run 'test'" (you will see your Python file name instead of *test*).

You will see the output in the "Run" section.

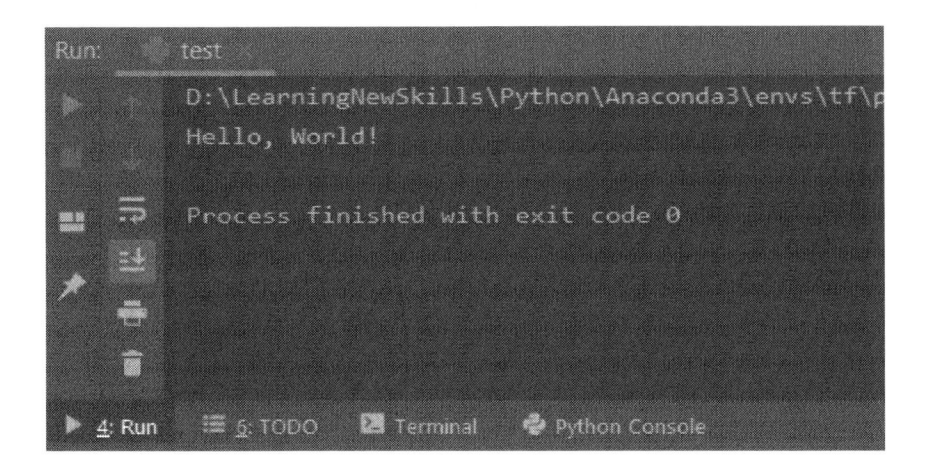

Other important thing to mention here is the "Terminal", which is the Windows command prompt, so you can perform system action without leaving PyCharm. Don't forget the "Python Console", that you can use to execute a single line of code, very useful for testing. There is also the "TODO", which is a to-do list for PyCharm; let's leave it for later.

"Process finished with exit code 0" is Python interpreter's way of telling us that everything worked without any errors. We can suppress this output, which we will look into that later.

We are going to come back to this "tensorENV" when we start with machine learning. Using the above steps, create a new virtual environment and call it "basics". Create a new project "Basics" and add the file "firstprog.py" in it.

We are going to print "Climate change is real!" 10 times.

for i in range(0, 11):

  print('Climate change is real!')

You will see the following output.

Climate change is real!

Climate change is real!

Climate change is real!

Climate change is real!

Climate change is real!

Climate change is real!

Climate change is real!

Climate change is real!

Climate change is real!

Climate change is real!

Climate change is real!

Process finished with exit code 0

We have used a "for" loop to perform an operation ("print()" method) several times. Another method used here is the range() that creates a sequence when given a starting and ending point. The example proves that range() stops the sequence one value short of the ending point (stopped at 10 when 11 was given as ending point).

We can do the same with a "while" loop which is beneficial in situations where we don't know beforehand how many times the operation must be performed.

```
i = 1



while i < 11:

    print('Climate change is real!')

    i += 1
```

Let's write a program to print a ladder of '#' to the number of levels user wants.

```
i = int(input('Enter the level of ladders you want to create: '))



for x in range(1, i+1):
```

```
spac = ' ' * (i-1)

char = '#' * x

print('%s%s' % (spac, char))

i -= 1
```

The output of the above code will be like below if user inputs 10.

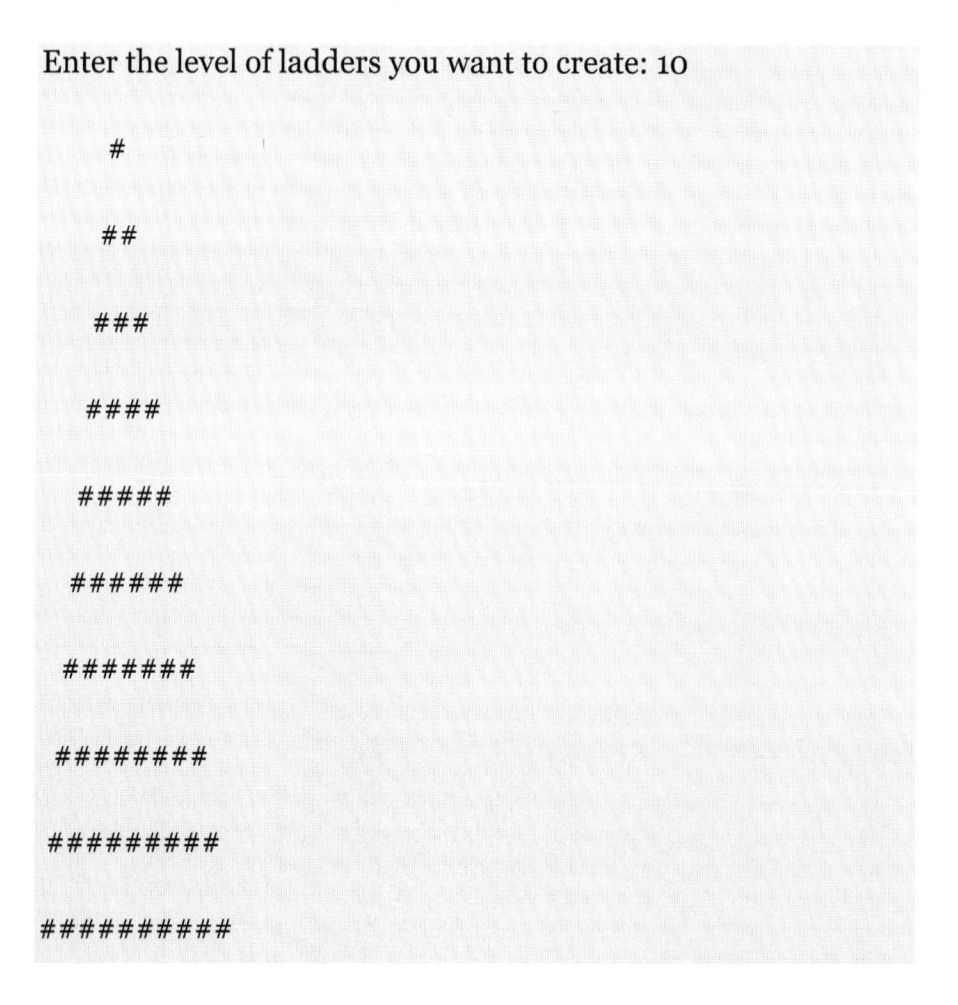

```
Enter the level of ladders you want to create: 10
         #
        ##
       ###
      ####
     #####
    ######
   #######
  ########
 #########
```

It looks more like a cone because space and "#" don't take up equal physical space in a word processor. In PyCharm, here's how the output looks.

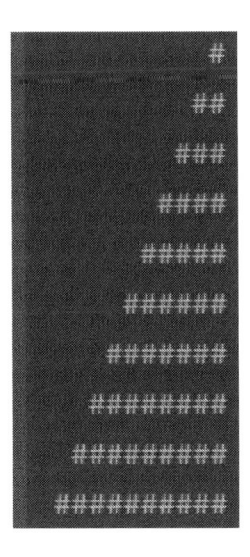

```
        #
       ##
      ###
     ####
    #####
   ######
  #######
 ########
#########
##########
```

In this script, we have involved the user using the input() method. We have used the int() to perform string to integer conversion because input() always registers the user input as a string. "i -= 1" is a short version of "i = i -1".

Data Structures

Lists and Tuples

Lists are the simplest data structure in Python, but that doesn't mean it's primitive.

aLst = [1, 3 , 5.55, 2, 4 ,6, 'numbers', 'are', 'not', 'letters'] print('Number of elements in the list: ', len(aLst))

for itm in aLst:

    print(itm)

The script will output the following.

Number of elements in the list: 10

1

3

5

2

4

6

numbers

are

not

letters

Let's do some more.

bLst = ['letters','are','forever',7,8,9]

```
cLst = aLst + bLst

print('Number of elements in the list: ', len(cLst))

for itm in cLst:

    print(itm)
```

The output is below.

1

3

5

2

4

6

numbers

are

not

letters

letters

are

forever

7

8

9

The "+" is an arithmetic operator, but by using it on two (or more) lists, it joins all the lists. There are many other ways of concatenating lists like join() and append(). In this script, we have used len() method to count the number of elements in a list. All data structures in Python are iterable, which is evident with the use of "for" loop on the list.

The order of elements in a list is fixed and governed by the order they are added/appended to the list, called index of that element. The first element of a list has zero index.

cLst[0]

1

clst[len(cLst)-1]

9

We can slice a list using the indices that returns a new list. As we will see soon, list is not the only data structure in Python to support slicing.

cLst[0:5] #will return elements with index of zero to index of four

[1, 3, 5, 2, 4]

A new element is always added at the end of the list.

cLst.append('New element')

print(cLst)

[1, 3, 5, 2, 4, 6, 'numbers', 'are', 'not', 'letters', 'letters', 'are', 'forever', 7, 8, 9, 'New element']

We can also remove elements from a list using various methods, including pop() where you can pass the index of the element you want to remove from the list. If no index is provided, the last element is removed.

cLst.pop()

print(cLst)

[1, 3, 5, 2, 4, 6, 'numbers', 'are', 'not', 'letters', 'letters', 'are', 'forever', 7, 8, 9]

Here is another reason why Python is so popular in data science applications, it is very smart with memory management. The biggest challenge for memory management is to handle duplication and decide when it's essential and when it's superfluous. Here is one example of Python's memory management in action.

cLst.append('New element') #add back the popped element

dLst = cLst

dLst.pop()

print(cLst)

print(dLst)

[1, 3, 5, 2, 4, 6, 'numbers', 'are', 'not', 'letters', 'letters', 'are', 'forever', 7, 8, 9]

[1, 3, 5, 2, 4, 6, 'numbers', 'are', 'not', 'letters', 'letters', 'are', 'forever', 7, 8, 9]

The assignment operators work a little differently in Python if applied to a data structure. Instead of creating two lists with identical elements, Python creates a new pointer "dLst" that points to the original list "cLst". "dLst.pop()" therefore changes the original list "cLst". We can say cLst and dLst are two names of the same entity.

The elements in a list can repeat.

```
dLst = [1, 1, 2, 3, 4, 5, 5]

print(dLst)

[1, 1, 2, 3, 4, 5, 5]
```

We can also reverse and sort a list.

```
eLst = [5,7,2,4,7889,7984,21,4,8]
```

print(list(reversed(dLst))) #get a new list with elements in reversed order but without sorting, doesn't modify the original list

eLst.sort(reverse=True) #descending sorting of list, modifies original list

print(eLst)

print(sorted(eLst)) #returns an ascending sorted list, doesn't modify original list

The above print methods will output the following, respectively:

[5, 5, 4, 3, 2, 1, 1]

[7984, 7889, 21, 8, 7, 5, 4, 4, 2]

[2, 4, 4, 5, 7, 8, 21, 7889, 7984]

Tuples are just like lists but have following distinctions

1. Tuples are unordered – elements don't have fixed position (index)
2. Tuples are immutable – elements can't be added or removed later

aTup = (1, 2, 3, 'first')

print(aTup)

(1, 2, 3, 'first')

Tuples don't support methods that change the tuple, which make them ideal for someone to pass information to others.

bTup = (3, 4, 5, 'second')

cTup = aTup + bTup

print(cTup)

(1, 2, 3, 'first', 3, 4, 5, 'second')

print(len(cTup)) #

8

print(cTup.count(3)) #count how many times "3" is in the tuple

2

print('first' in cTup) #check if "first" is an element of the tuple

True

We can create new tuples out of existing ones.

dTup = (2, 5, 33, 5, 7)

eTup = tuple(reversed(dTup))

print(eTup)

The output is.

(7, 5, 33, 5, 2)

Strings

Strings are an immutable collection of characters. Strings are a basic data type in Python but also behave like a data structure (list). This is the reason many data structure methods are applicable on strings. One of the reasons Python has taken over as the best data analysis programming language is the ease it offers in manipulating strings.

aStr = "This is a\nsimple string"

bStr = r"This is a\nraw string. Special characters like \n are taken as simple characters."

print(aStr)

print(bStr)

The above will result in the following output:

This is a

simple string

This is a\nraw string. Special characters like \n are taken as simple characters.

Note how the first string takes two lines because the "\n" is taken as a newline.

We have already seen that when taking input from the user, the input data is always taken as a string, and in some cases, we have to perform type conversion to get the correct data.

inp = input("Enter a number: ")

print(type(inp))

Here is a test of the above code.

Enter a number: 110

<class 'str'>

Even though the input looks like a number, it isn't, and we have to convert to integer.

inp = int(inp)

Likewise, we can convert other data types into string.

intNum = 245

cStr = str(intNum)

print(type(cStr), cStr)

The output will be.

<class 'str'> 245

Let's perform some data structure operations on a string.

get number of characters in a string

print(len(aStr))

print(len(bStr))

get specific character using its index

print(aStr[len(aStr)-1]) #last character of aStr

slicing a string to get a new string

print(aStr[0:4]) #last index is exclusive

print(aStr[-6:]) #negative indices can be used

The respective outputs will be.

23

81

g

This

string

Now, a few methods specific to the string data type.

some string specific methods

print(aStr.lower()) #returns new string with all lowercase letters

print(cStr.strip()) #removes whitespace from start and end of string

print(aStr.replace("\n"," ")) #replaced newline with a space

print(bStr.split(r"\n")) #creates a list of substrings, note the "\n" passed as a raw string

print("<missing>".join(bStr.split(r"\n"))) #join a list to create a string

print(aStr + bStr) #concatenate two strings

print("\"%s\" is a string" %bStr)

The respective outputs are below.

this is a

simple string

This is another string

This is a simple string

['This is a', 'raw string. Special characters like ', ' are taken as simple characters.']

This is a<missing>raw string. Special characters like <missing> are taken as simple characters.

This is a

simple stringThis is a\nraw string. Special characters like \n are taken as simple characters.

"This is a\nraw string. Special characters like \n are taken as simple characters." is a string

We can also use a loop on a string.

for char in aStr:

    print(char, end=" == ")

The output is.

T== h== i== s== == i== s== == a==

== s== i== m== p== l== e== == s== t== r== i== n== g==

Dictionaries

A very unique key-value pair data structure, dictionaries are mutable, ordered, and iterable.

aDict = {

    "a":"A member",

    "b":"B member",

    0:[2, 4, 6],

    1:[3, 5, 7]

}

print(aDict["a"])

print(aDict[0])

print(aDict[0][2])

The output is.

A member

[2, 4, 6]

6

Let's change a value and then a key.

aDict["a"] = "First member"

print(aDict["a"])

aDict["1st"] = aDict.pop("a")

print(aDict)

The output for both print methods is below.

First member

{'b': 'B member', 0: [2, 4, 6], 1: [3, 5, 7], '1st': 'First member'}

Note, the new key-value pair now appears at the end of the dictionary.

We can get all the keys and values as separate lists from a dictionary.

print(aDict.keys())

print(aDict.values())

The output is a little strange-looking, see below.

dict_keys(['a', 'b', 0, 1])

dict_values(['A member', 'B member', [2, 4, 6], [3, 5, 7]])

The "dict_keys" and "dict_values" are view objects and don't reside in the memory. You can say they are merely references to the original dictionary. You cannot iterate over these view objects, but you can check membership.

print('B member' in aDict.values())

The output is.

True

Checking if a key is in a dictionary is simpler.

print("a" in aDict)

The output is.

True

If we try to get a value using a key that is not present in a dictionary, an error occurs.

print(aDict["c"])

The output will be.

KeyError: 'c'

There is a safe method, get(). If the key is not found, the default message is returned instead of raising an error.

print(aDict.get("c","Key not found"))

The output will be.

Key not found

Sets

A dictionary with only keys and no values is called a set. This is the closest you will get to mathematical sets in Python. Sets are mutable, iterable, unordered, and all elements must be unique. Because the sets are unordered, the set elements don't have fixed indices; therefore, retrieving elements with indices and slicing doesn't work.

aSet = {'data collection', 'data analysis', 'data visualization'}

bSet = set([1, 2, 3])

cSet = {1, 1, 2, 3}

print(aSet)

print(bSet)

print(cSet)

print(2 in bSet)

print((bSet == cSet)) #ignored duplicate element leading to cSet and bSet having the same elements

The output of the above code will be.

{'data collection', 'data analysis', 'data visualization'}

{1, 2, 3}

{1, 2, 3}

True

True

Let's see what more we can do with sets.

#set operations

print(bSet & cSet) #set intersection – return common elements

print(aSet | bSet) #set union – join sets

print(bSet - cSet) #set difference – return elements of bSet that are not in cSet, null set in this case

cSet.add(4) #add a single element, ignored if element already present in the set

print(cSet)

cSet.remove(4) #raises error if element is not found in the set, differs from pop() as it doesn't return the removed element

print(cSet)

cSet.discard(4) #ignored if element isn't found in the set instead of raising an error

nums = [4, 5, 6]

cSct.update(nums) #adds multiple elements to the set at the same time

print(cSet)

cSet.clear() #removes all elements making the set empty

print(cSet)

The output is.

{1, 2, 3}

{'data visualization', 1, 2, 'data collection', 3, 'data analysis'}

set()

{1, 2, 3, 4}

{1, 2, 3}

{1, 2, 3, 4, 5, 6}

set()

Advanced Programming

Python is a high-level language that offers various distinct functionalities such as comprehensions and iterators. But, first, let's look at how to create functions and handle exceptions.

Creating and Using Functions

Functions are code blocks that are explicitly called to perform specific tasks. They can, optionally, take single or multiple inputs and return a single output. The best practice is that a function should not have more than two inputs (also called function arguments). The single output can be a data structure if more than one value needs to be returned.

Here is a complete script with the function "checkodd()" that takes an array of integer numbers and decides if each element is odd or even.

```python
def checkodd(num):

    arr = []

    for itr in num:

        if(itr%2 != 0):

            arr.append(str(itr))

    return arr
```

```
def main():

    inputArr = []

    for i in range(1, 11):

        inp = int(input("Enter an integer number: "))

        inputArr.append(inp)

    oddNums = checkodd(inputArr)

    print("The odd numbers in the user inputs are: ", ", ".join(oddNums))


if __name__ == "__main__":

    main()
```

Here is the result of a test I did.

Enter an integer number: 3

Enter an integer number: 5

Enter an integer number: 4

Enter an integer number: 2

Enter an integer number: 6

Enter an integer number: 9

Enter an integer number: 8

Enter an integer number: 7

Enter an integer number: 12

Enter an integer number: 31

The odd numbers in the user inputs are: 3, 5, 9, 7, 31

Let's discuss the different aspects of this code.

The definition of a function should appear before it's call. It's not a requirement but rather a good practice rule. I had to pass 10 inputs to the function, so I combined all the inputs in an array and passed to the function. I applied the same logic to the function return.

The "if __name__ == "__main__":" is where the execution of the script starts. You can say it acts like a pointer because every script you write can be imported into another script as a module. In that case, Python needs to know where the script execution should start.

This a very simple example where we could have achieved the results without writing a custom function.

Variable Scope

When writing functions, it's important to understand the scope of a variable. It means where you have declared a variable and where it's available. A variable can be either local or global depending upon where they are declared.

In the above script, "arr" is a local variable (list) of function checkodd(). If we try to access it from main() function, we will get an error. In the same way, the list "inputArr" is local to the main() function, if we try to access it from checkodd(), we will get an error. Here's a benefit of using PyCharm. If you try to access a variable that isn't available in a function, PyCharm will give an error warning.

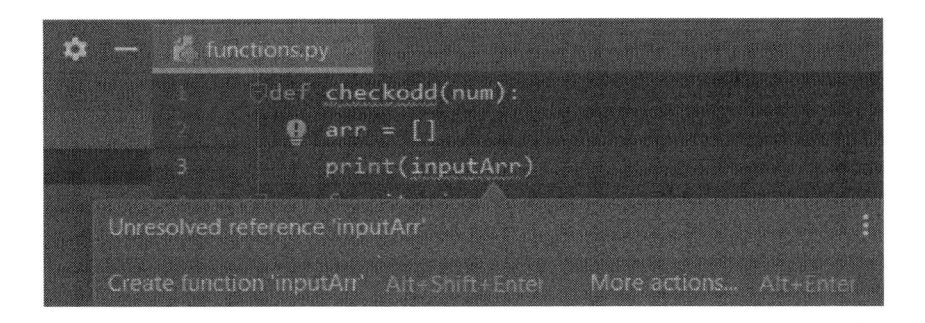

```
def checkodd(num):
    arr = []
    print(inputArr)
```
Unresolved reference 'inputArr'

If, we do want to access a variable across functions, we have to explicitly declare it as a global variable. To access "inputArr" inside checkodd() function definition, we have to change the main() definition to below.

def main():

    global inputArr #making the variable global

```
inputArr = [] #declaring it an empty list, unfortunately, we cannot declare the values and scope of the variable in the same line

    for i in range(1, 11):

        inp = int(input("Enter an integer number: "))

        inputArr.append(inp)

    oddNums = checkodd(inputArr)

    print("The odd numbers in the user inputs are: ", ", ".join(oddNums))
```

If you don't want to use the "global" keyword, we have to relocate the "inputArr" declaration to the top of the script. Here's the complete updated script.

```
inputArr = []


def checkodd(num):

    arr = []

    print(inputArr)

    for itr in num:

        if(itr%2 != 0):
```

arr.append(str(itr))

return arr

def main():

for i in range(1, 11):

inp = int(input("Enter an integer number: "))

inputArr.append(inp)

oddNums = checkodd(inputArr)

print("The odd numbers in the user inputs are: ", ", ".join(oddNums))

if __name__ == "__main__":

main()

The output now, with some random inputs below.

Enter an integer number: 45

Enter an integer number: 2

Enter an integer number: 36

Enter an integer number: 785

Enter an integer number: 1

Enter an integer number: 5

Enter an integer number: 2

Enter an integer number: 3

Enter an integer number: 5

Enter an integer number: 7

[45, 2, 36, 785, 1, 5, 2, 3, 5, 7]

The odd numbers in the user inputs are: 45, 785, 1, 5, 3, 5, 7

List Comprehensions

In previous examples, we have used loops to iterate over a list. Python offers a faster way that's more powerful than using a loop on a list in many situations. It is called list comprehension.

Let's create a function to populate an empty list with prime numbers between 1 and 100.

```
import math

primeNums = []



def populatePrime(num):
```

```
        max_divizr = 1 + math.floor(math.sqrt(num))

        for divizr in range(2, max_divizr):

                if(num % divizr == 0):

                        return

        primeNums.append(str(num))

        return


def main():

        for i in range(2, 101):

                populatePrime(i)

        print("The prime numbers between 1 and 100 are: ", ", ".join(primeNums))


if __name__ == "__main__":

        main()
```

The script imports a standard library in Python "maths" to implement a faster algorithm to find prime numbers in a given range. Mathematically, we know that an integer cannot be a prime number if it's divisible by a number less than or equal to its square root. We also know that range() never includes the maximum value given. We have declared a global list "primeNums" to collect the prime numbers. We can make the code more dynamic by adding an input() asking the user to enter the maximum range the prime numbers should be found in. We have to change the main() function definition to below.

```python
def main():

    inp = int(input("Enter an integer number. The prime numbers will be output up until this number: ")) + 1

    for i in range(2, inp):

        populatePrime(i)

    print("The prime numbers between 1 and 100 are: ", ", ".join(primeNums))
```

Notice the one we added to the user input to get the correct maximum range value with the variable "inp".

We can use list comprehensions instead of using the nested for-if in the populatePrime() function. Here's the updated function definition.

```python
import math


def populatePrime(num):
```

```python
        return [str(x) for x in range(2, num) if all(x % y for y in range(2, 1 + math.floor(math.sqrt(x))))]


def main():

    inp = int(input("Enter an integer number. The prime numbers will be output up till this number: "))

    primeNums = populatePrime(inp)

    print("The prime numbers between 1 and 100 are: ", ", ".join(primeNums))


if __name__ == "__main__":

    main()
```

The output of the above code if user enters 100 is.

Enter an integer number. The prime numbers will be output up till this number: 100

The prime numbers between 1 and 100 are: 2, 3, 5, 7, 11, 13, 17, 19, 23, 29, 31, 37, 41, 43, 47, 53, 59, 61, 67, 71, 73, 79, 83, 89, 97

As you can see, the results are the same. List comprehensions offer, in most cases, faster execution times but are very hard to read for people who are new to Python. This is evident from the below line of code.

[str(x) for x in range(2, num) if all(x % y for y in range(2, 1 + math.floor(math.sqrt(x))))]

You don't have to use list comprehensions if you don't want to, but when dealing with large data sets, the execution times do matter.

Revisiting Mathematical Concepts

Vectors

An object with magnitude and specific direction is called a vector. We can visualize a vector as an arrow figure whose length represents the magnitude and the arrowhead indicating its direction. The opposite of vector quantities are scalar quantities that have only magnitude.

One of the easiest examples of scalar and vector quantities is speed and velocity. For example, a car is travelling 50 kilometers every hour towards south. The speed of the car is 13.89 m/s and it's velocity is 50 km/hr North.

[Diagram: a vector arrow labeled with "head" at the tip, "tail" at the base, "magnitude" along its length, and "direction" indicating its orientation.]

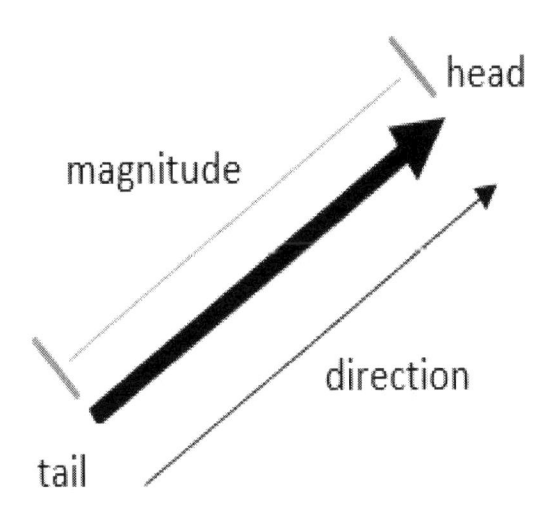

There is one unique vector that doesn't have a particular direction, the zero vector. Represented with a bolded **o**, the zero vector has zero magnitude and doesn't point in a specific direction.

Why are vectors important? Let's consider distance vs. displacement. Without direction, distance covered doesn't portray the complete story. You might have traveled 10 kms to the mall and 10 kms back to your home, travelling a total distance of 20 kms. But, your displacement is zero because you ended up where you started. It is this reason displacement is always used for navigational purposes.

Vector Operations

Moving a vector while keeping its magnitude and direction intact is called translation. Translation doesn't change a vector and helps in performing vector operations.

Addition

To add two vectors **a** and **b**, which is written as **a** + **b**, we translate vector **b** so its tail touches the head of vector **a**. Now, join the tail of vector **a** with the head of vector **b**, this new vector shows the result of **a** + **b**.

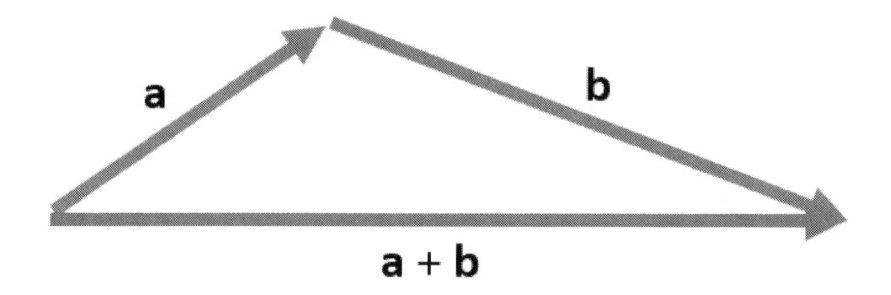

Addition operation obeys the cumulative law; it means the order of operators doesn't matter.

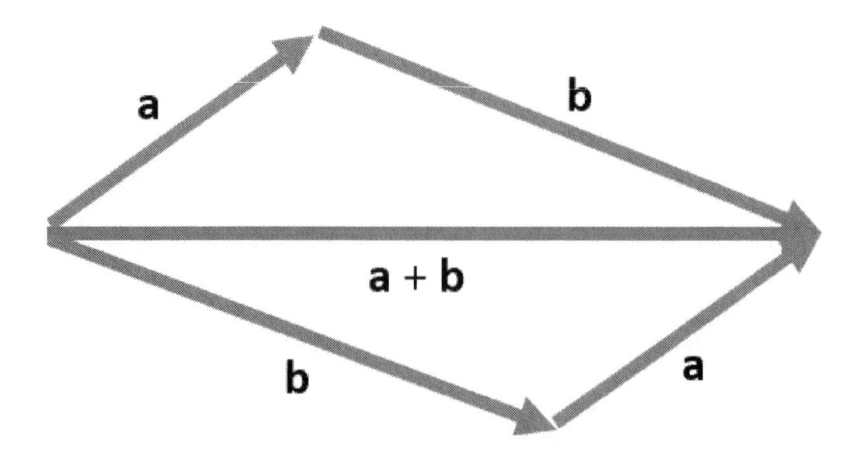

Subtraction

Subtraction is also addition between two vectors but direction of the second vector is reversed. So, to calculate **b** - **a**, we actually perform **b** + (**-a**).

Scalar Multiplication

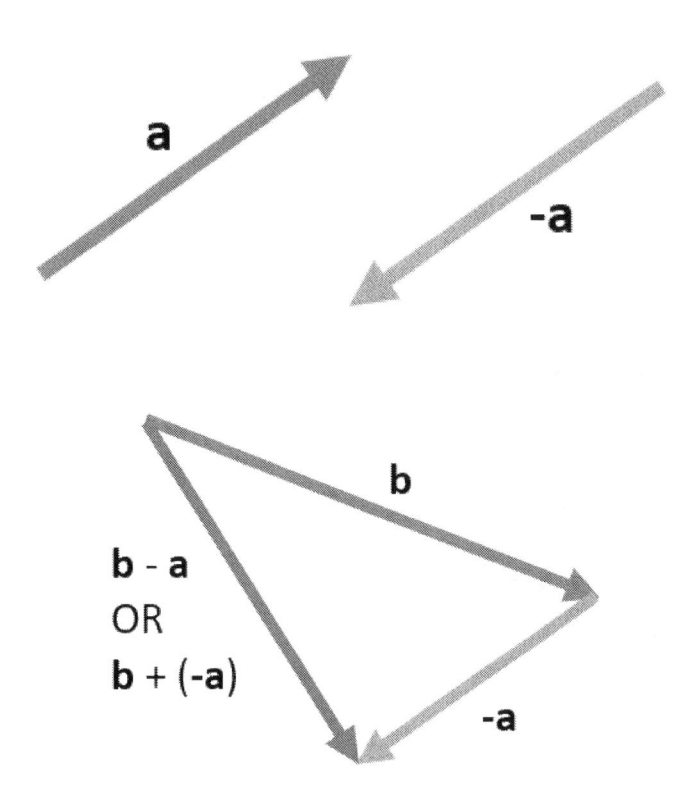

Scalar multiplication is multiplying a vector with a real number (called scalar). The direction of the vector remains the same but the magnitude of the vector increases by the scalar value.

Vector Multiplication

There are two different types of vector multiplication, dot product and cross product.

Dot product is used to find how much one vector is in the same direction as another vector. Dot product doesn't have anything to do with the magnitude of the vectors. A positive result means both vectors have similar direction; zero indicates both vectors are perpendicular; while a negative results shows both vectors have almost opposite direction. Dot product always return only a number.

Cross product of two vectors results in a new vector that is perpendicular to the vectors and a magnitude equal to the area of parallelogram created by the two vectors. If two vectors are parallel, the cross product is zero, and if the vectors are perpendicular, the cross product is maximum. The direction of the new vector can be easily found using the right hand rule. If you point your index and middle fingers in the direction of two vectors, the direction of your upright thumb represents the direction of new vector.

Matrices

An arrangement of numbers, symbols, and/or their combinations in rows and columns forming a rectangular array is called matrix. A matrix with 3 rows and 3 columns with all elements equal to one is written as follows.

$$\begin{bmatrix} 1 & 1 & 1 \\ 1 & 1 & 1 \\ 1 & 1 & 1 \end{bmatrix}$$

Matrix Operations

Various scalar operations including addition and subtraction can be performed on a matrix. A matrix can also be operated along with another matrix.

$$\begin{bmatrix} 17 & 6 \\ 3 & 4 \end{bmatrix}$$

"17" and "4" comprise the primary diagonal while "6" and "3" comprise the secondary diagonal.

Identity Matrix

A square matrix that has all elements in primary diagonal set as one and all elements in the secondary diagonal set as zero is called an identity matrix. Here is a 2x2 identity matrix.

$$\begin{bmatrix} 1 & 0 \\ 0 & 1 \end{bmatrix}$$

Scalar Multiplication

If a matrix is multiplied by a number, it's called scalar multiplication.

$$3 \times \begin{bmatrix} 1 & 1 & 1 \\ 1 & 1 & 1 \\ 1 & 1 & 1 \end{bmatrix} = \begin{bmatrix} 3 & 3 & 3 \\ 3 & 3 & 3 \\ 3 & 3 & 3 \end{bmatrix}$$

Matrix Addition

We can add two matrices which requires both matrices to have same number of rows and columns. The element of one matrix is added with the element of the other matrix with the corresponding position.

$$\begin{bmatrix} 1 & 2 & 3 \\ 4 & 5 & 6 \\ 7 & 8 & 9 \end{bmatrix} + \begin{bmatrix} 9 & 8 & 7 \\ 6 & 5 & 4 \\ 3 & 2 & 1 \end{bmatrix} = \begin{bmatrix} 10 & 10 & 10 \\ 10 & 10 & 10 \\ 10 & 10 & 10 \end{bmatrix}$$

Matrix Multiplication

Two matrices can be multiplied only if the number of columns of first matrix is equal to the number of rows of second matrix. The resultant matrix will have a number of rows of first matrix and number of columns of second matrix.

$$\begin{bmatrix} 2 & 5 & -9 \\ 17 & 5 & 1 \end{bmatrix} \times \begin{bmatrix} 2 & 4 \\ 3 & 5 \\ 1 & 1 \end{bmatrix} = \begin{bmatrix} 10 & 24 \\ 50 & 94 \end{bmatrix}$$

Matrix Determinant

Determinant is a special characteristic of a matrix that helps in various applications such as finding the inverse of a matrix to solve some linear equations. The matrix must be square, i.e., same number of rows and columns. The determinant can be zero. Let's consider the below matrix.

$$\begin{bmatrix} 17 & 6 \\ 3 & 4 \end{bmatrix}$$

The determinant of this matrix is found by multiplying elements in the secondary diagonal and subtracting the result from the multiplication of elements in the primary diagonal. The operation gives the determinant of the above matrix as: 17 x 4 - 6 x 3 = 50.

Matrix Inversion

If the determinant of a matrix is zero, we cannot find its inverse. In all other cases, we reciprocate the determinant and multiply by the adjugate of the original matrix. To find the adjugate of a matrix, we swap the position of elements in primary diagonal and change the signs of elements in secondary diagonal.

$$I = \frac{1}{50} \begin{bmatrix} 4 & -6 \\ -3 & 17 \end{bmatrix}$$

$$I = \begin{bmatrix} 4/50 & -6/50 \\ -3/50 & 17/50 \end{bmatrix}$$

If we multiply the above matrix with the original matrix, we will get an identity matrix.

Bonus: we can write a vector as a single column or single row matrix. This way, all matrix operations can be applied to vectors.

Matrix Transpose

Transposing a matrix involves switching the elements in the rows to columns. Let's consider the following matrix.

$$\begin{bmatrix} 2 & 5 & -9 \\ 17 & 5 & 1 \end{bmatrix}$$

The transpose of the above matrix is.

$$\begin{bmatrix} 2 & 17 \\ 5 & 5 \\ -9 & 1 \end{bmatrix}$$

Basic Statistics

You cannot perform data analysis and machine learning without basic statistics. In most machine-learning applications, you train your script to analyze an entire data set through a single, yet varying perspective and find related potential predictors. The statistics that involves a single variate/variable is called univariate statistics.

Univariate statistics are largely based on linear models which are heavily involved in machine learning.

Outlier

Have you ever thought about the concept of superheroes? People among us (the data set) but very different? So much different that they outside the characteristic boundaries of all else. An average untrained American male can lift around 155 lbs. How much superman can lift? According to the comics, 2 billion tons! If we include superman in the calculation of how much an average American male can lift, the result will not be truly representative of the general population (data set).

Detecting outliers in a data set and what to do with them is very important. In most cases, outliers are discarded because they don't represent the data set correctly. This is because outliers usually happen due to an error while gathering data. But, that's not always the case. Let's take an example. An industrial oven bakes cookies, and a sensor is used to monitor the oven's temperature. The oven has two doors; Door A is used to feed cookie dough into the oven while Door B is used to takeout baked cookies. The sensor records the temperature in Fahrenheit every second. Here are the readings.

349.5, 350.5, 350.1, 350, 150, 348.5, 349, 350, 349.5, 149.25, 351.5, 350, 349.5, 350.1, 149.7

Something strange is happening; every 5 seconds, the temperature drops well below the desired temperature range to bake cookies (ideally the temperature should be 350°F). There can be two possibilities:

1. The sensor is malfunctioning.
2. Heat is leaking.

1 is a possibility, but the data is too precise to indicate any malfunction. The temperature drops every 5 seconds like clockwork. 2 is a greater possibility, but why is it happening all the time? Something must be happening every 5 seconds to cause this heat loss. After some careful process investigation, it was found that the temperature drops steeply because both the oven doors, A and B, are opened at the same time. Opening both the doors by a few seconds apart resolves the issue to a great extent.

Average

The concept of average is to find the centerpoint of a data set. Why? The centerpoint of a data set tells a lot about the important characteristics of the data set.

Mean

The most common average is the mean. It is calculated by summing all the elements in a data set and dividing that sum by the number of elements in the data set. Remember when we said "an average untrained American male can lift around 155 lbs?" It was a mean of the weight lifted by a specific number of untrained American males. Mean gives as a general idea of the entire data set.

349.5, 350.5, 350.1, 350, 150, 348.5, 349, 350, 349.5, 149.25, 351.5, 350, 349.5, 350.1, 149.7

These were the temperatures recorded every second in an industrial oven. How to calculate the mean? We add all the readings and divide by the number of readings. The mean comes up as 4647.15/15 = 309.81°F. The temperature should have remained around 350°F for the best results.

Median

Median represents the true center by position in a data set. The data set is first sorted in ascending order. If the data set has an odd number of values, the median is the value that has an equal number of values on both sides. Let's find the median in our industrial oven example. First, we sort the data set in ascending order.

149.25, 149.7, 150, 348.5, 349, 349.5, 349.5, 349.5, 350, 350, 350, 350.1, 350.1, 350.5, 351.5

There are 15 recorded values which is an odd number. The median in this case is 349.5, the value at 8th position because it has an equal number of values (7) on both sides. If we had an even number of values, we would have to calculate the mean of the two values that have an equal number of values on both sides. For example, here's how many kilometers I drove every day for the last eight days.

101, 215, 52, 87, 64, 33, 459, 16

Let's sort the data set.

16, 33, 52, 64, 87, 101, 215, 459

The two middle values are 64 and 87. The median in this case is (64+87) / 2 = 75.5 kms

Mode

The most repeated (common) value in a data set is called mode. If none of the values repeat, the data set doesn't have a mode. In our industrial oven example, 350 appears three times and hence is the mode of the data set.

Variance

It is the measure of variability of each value in the data set with respect to its mean. It is used in investments and revenues to optimize various assets to achieve a target average. Let's take an example. You have a physical store, an online store and a kiosk in the mall. Your physical store generates a revenue of $30k a month, your online store generates a revenue of $24k a month and the kiosk generates $12k a month. Your average revenue is $22k each month. To see which asset contributes more to your average revenue, we use the formula:

sum of (asset revenue - mean revenue)² / number of assets.

For our stores, the variance is, ((30 - 22)² + (24 - 22)² + (12 - 22)²) / 3 = 56

The lower the variance the lesser away the individual revenue contributions are from the average revenue.

Standard Deviation

We find standard deviation by taking the square root of variance. For the above example, the standard deviation is 7.48. Standard deviation shows what's the extent of deviation of the data set as a whole from its mean.

Probability

The likelihood or chance of something to happen is called probability. In machine learning, probability is one of the most important concepts at play. In most real-world scenarios, it is impossible to tell what will happen next accurately. It is this reason, whenever we talk about future events, we talk about the likelihood of something happening. A simple example is the weather forecast where the weatherperson suggests or expects something might happen, but many times it doesn't happen the same way.

There are events where probability doesn't apply; for example, universal truths like the sun will always rise in the morning (unless the world is going to end). Probability only makes sense for events (or experiments) where more than one outcome can occur. The probability of such an event can be expressed mathematically as:

Probability = number of ways an outcome can happen / total number of possible outcomes

Probability lies between zero and one; zero meaning there's zero chance and one meaning something is imminent. It also means probability is never negative. The events or experiments should be repeatable infinite amount of times without any external interference.

Another important thing to remember is that finding probability in each event may or may not affect the probability found in the consecutive events. For example, when flipping a coin, there's an equal 50% chance (0.5 probability) the outcome will be either a head or a tail. If we get a head on the first flip, that doesn't mean on the next flip that we are going to get a tail. The probability again resets to 50% for either a heads or tails outcome on each flip (or event or experiment as its generally called).

So, is there an example where each consecutive event changes the probability of the next event? Yes, there is. Let's the example of a complete deck of 52 cards. There are four ace cards, 12 face cards and 36 number cards. Let's shuffle the cards so there's randomness and fairness in the system. What is the probability of drawing an ace from the deck? In the first draw, the probability is 4/52. Assume that the card drawn was Queen of Hearts, if we perform a second draw without putting this Queen card back in the deck, the total possibilities reduce to 51 in the second draw. The probability of drawing an ace is now 4/51. If no ace is drawn even after 12 draws and not putting the drawn card back in the deck, the probability of drawing an ace on the thirteenth draw will be 4/40. This is an example of a simple system where the probability of an occurrence changes with each event.

Distribution

Distribution can be of many types, but for this book, whenever we talk about distribution, we are talking about probability distribution unless explicitly stated otherwise. Let's consider an example.

We are going to flip a coin three times, taken as one event, and record the outcome. We will repeat the process until we have all the possible unique outcomes. Here's a list of all unique outcomes. H H H

H H T

H T H

T H H

H T T

T H T

T T H

T T T What is the probability of finding exactly one head? We look at the possible outcomes and count all the outcomes that have exactly one head. Out of total eight possible outcomes, we have three possibilities of getting exactly one head, which makes the probability ⅜. What's the probability of getting zero heads? It is ⅛. Three heads? Also, ⅛. Two heads? The same as one head, which is ⅜.

This is a simple example with a very small set of total possible outcomes. It is easier to understand the different probabilities as fractions. But, consider a data set that has millions of possible outcomes, which is the case in most real-life scenarios. The fractions become too complex to understand. To make the probability of different possible outcomes easier to understand, the probability distributions are created. It is a visual representation that makes more sense than looking at fractions.

Our current events are random yet discreet because only known values can occur. The probability distribution is referred to as discrete. If we denote the event as X, the following chart represents the discrete probability distribution of random variable X.

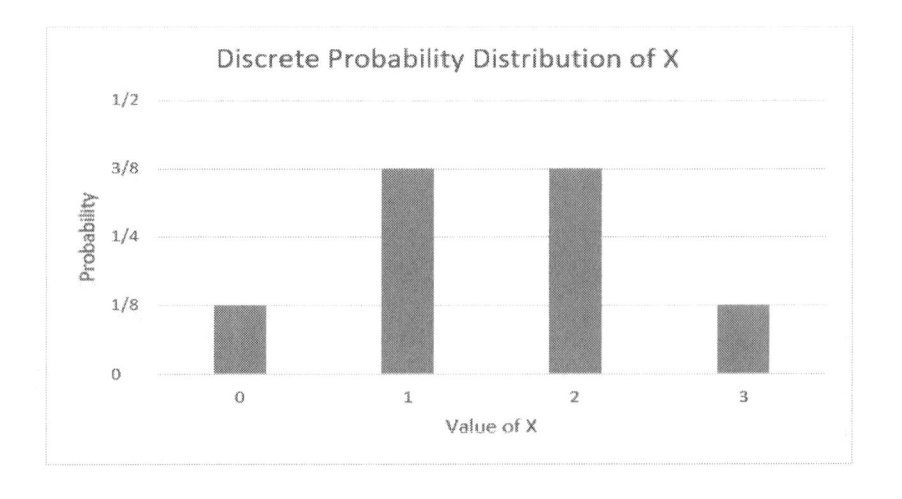

Discrete Probability Distribution of X

Value of X	Probability
0	1/8
1	3/8
2	3/8
3	1/8

Data Analysis – Foundation of Machine Learning

Before we do machine learning, we have to perform data analysis. There are various stages in data analysis. For machine learning, we only require data munging, but still, it's a good idea to learn about data analysis before learning about machine learning.

In simple terms, if the data is analyzed to understand what happened in the past, the process is data analysis. If that analysis is built upon to predict what's going to happen in the future, it's machine learning. There are many overlapping concepts, and you can't separate one from the other.

Let's setup a project "data_analysis" in PyCharm, and we will start coding with some basic data analysis.

Python Libraries for Data Analysis

Python provides a lot of libraries to source data depending upon its origin. The biggest power of data analysis libraries is they support reading data from the most common data sources by default. It means we don't need another library to just read data. Let's start with our first data analysis library, NumPy, which are used to create multi-dimensional data structures called "numpy arrays."

NumPy

import numpy as np

aArr = np.array([40.71, 74.01])

bArr = np.array([[91, 7, -14],

[3, 5, -7]])

print(aArr.ndim) #get dimension of array

print(bArr.ndim) #note that when creating multidimensional arrays, the number of elements in each subarray must be the same

The output of the above script is:

1

2

You can say the "ndim" gives the number of rows in a numpy array. We can get the number of rows and columns using the shape.

print(aArr.shape) #returns a tuple of rows and columns, for one-dimensional array, only the number of columns are returned print(bArr.shape)

The output is:

(2,)

(2, 3)

You might say we can do all that with nested lists. Even though numpy arrays look like nested lists, we can do much more with them.

To get the number of elements in a numpy array, we can use the following code:

print(bArr.size) #outputs 6 as there are total 6 elements in the bArr

We can use indices to access individual elements. Just like lists, the indices of a numpy array start from zero but with a little bit different syntax.

print(bArr[0,2]) #outputs -14

Notice the difference, if it would have been a nested list, we would have used "bArr[0][2]" to access -14.

Unlike lists, all the elements in a numpy array must be of same data type. If not, numpy will try to convert all elements to the same data type, which is usually string.

cArr = np.array([123, "is a", " number", True])

print(cArr)

The output will be:

['123' 'is a' ' number' 'True']

All the non-string values are converted to string. This is dangerous because during data munging, if we program to look for boolean True, our script will always fail for this array. Another observation, the commas are missing! Does this have to do with numpy changing the data types of the values? Let's print the other numpy arrays to check.

print(aArr)

print(bArr)

[40.71 74.01]

[[91 7 -14]

 [3 5 -7]]

So, this is the general behavior when printing the contents of an array. A little bit more on the conversion, our array already had two strings in it. What if we have an array that only has numbers and a boolean value?

dArr = np.array([555, True, False])

print(dArr)

The output is:

[555 1 0]

The boolean values were converted to the most similar number valuc.

Numpy arrays are immutable. Once created, we cannot add new values, remove existing ones or swap values. However, we can create new arrays from existing ones and make necessary changes during the process.

eArr = np.append(aArr, 555.55)

print(eArr)

The output is:

[40.71 74.01 555.55]

One more thing, any trailing zeros from a floating number are removed.

fArr = np.array([20.5, 14.00])

print(fArr)

The output is:

[20.5 14.]

What if we want to append data in a multidimensional array?

gArr = np.append(bArr[0], 4) #new array is one dimensional

print(gArr)

bArr = np.append(bArr, 4) #converts multidimensional array to one dimensional array

print(bArr)

The outputs are:

[91 7 -14 4]

[91 7 -14 3 5 -7 4]

We can also remove values that also results in a new array.

gArr = np.delete(gArr, 3) #takes the index of element to be removed. 3 is index of 4 in gArr

print(gArr)

The output is:

[91 7 -14]

The numpy library also facilitates in quickly creating commonly used arrays.

zArr = np.zeros((2, 3)) #by default the data type is floating

print(zArr)

zArr2 = np.zeros((2, 3), dtype=int)

print(zArr2)

The outputs are:

[[0. 0. 0.]

 [0. 0. 0.]]

[[0 0 0]

 [0 0 0]]

We can create a 3D array.

oArr = np.ones((2, 4, 4)) #read as multidimensional (3D) array containing two arrays each of 4 rows and 4 columns

print(oArr)

The output is:

[[[1. 1. 1. 1.]

 [1. 1. 1. 1.]

 [1. 1. 1. 1.]

 [1. 1. 1. 1.]]

[[1. 1. 1. 1.]

[1. 1. 1. 1.]

[1. 1. 1. 1.]

[1. 1. 1. 1.]]]

We can also create arrays with elements having a specific sequence.

seqArr = np.arange(0, 257, 32) #create sequence by telling how much space (step) should be between each element

print(seqArr)

linArr = np.linspace(0,256,9, dtype=int) #create sequence by telling number of elements needed. numpy sets the appropriate step

print(linArr)

The outputs are:

[0 32 64 96 128 160 192 224 256]

[0 32 64 96 128 160 192 224 256]

A few points to note about "linspace()":

1. The maximum extreme is included in the sequence

2. If we don't specify the data type, the sequence will have the default floating type

What if we want to create an array with all elements having the same value? We have a method for that as well.

samArr = np.full((3,3), 13)

print(samArr)

The code outputs the following:

[[13 13 13]

[13 13 13]

[13 13 13]]

We can also create an identity matrix.

idArr = np.eye(3, dtype=int) #identity matrices are always square, meaning the same number of rows and columns hence providing single value for both

print(idArr)

The output is:

[[1 0 0]

[0 1 0]

[0 0 1]]

We can also create arrays with random integers and floating numbers.

ranIntArr = np.random.randint(2, 16, size=(3, 3)) #2 and 16 are limits so numbers will be generated randomly between this range. (3, 3) is the size of matrix returned

print(ranIntArr)

ranFltArr = np.random.random((3, 3)) #generate a 3x3 square matrix with random float numbers

print(ranFltArr)

The outputs are (since we are using random methods, you might see different numbers when you execute the above code):

[[3 14 6]

 [10 10 4]

 [2 13 3]]

[[0.34134875 0.2531188 0.83863728]

 [0.78300571 0.47987474 0.88471375]

 [0.69181843 0.17512459 0.70456541]]

Let's perform some operations with numpy arrays.

```python
aArr = np.array([
    [2, 4, 6],
    [6, 4, 2]
])

bArr = np.array([
    [3, 5, 7],
    [7, 5, 3]
])

#addition
print(np.add(aArr, bArr)) #also aArr + bArr

#subtraction
print(np.subtract(aArr, bArr)) #also aArr - bArr

#multiplication - not matrix multiplication
print(np.multiply(aArr, bArr)) #also aArr * bArr
```

```
#division

print(np.divide(aArr, bArr)) #also aArr / bArr
```

The output of the above script is:

```
[[ 5  9 13]

 [13  9  5]]

[[-1 -1 -1]

 [-1 -1 -1]]

[[ 6 20 42]

 [42 20  6]]

[[0.66666667 0.8        0.85714286]

 [0.85714286 0.8        0.66666667]]
```

We can also perform dot and cross products on arrays.

```
cArr = np.array([

    [2, 4, 6],

    [6, 4, 2],

    [8, 9, 1]

])
```

```
dArr = np.array([
    [3, 5, 7],
    [7, 5, 3],
    [8, 9, 1]
])
#dot product
print(np.dot(cArr, dArr))

#cross product
print(np.cross(cArr, dArr))
```

The outputs are:

[[82 84 32]

 [62 68 56]

 [95 94 84]]

[[-2 4 -2]

 [2 -4 2]

 [0 0 0]]

Transposing an array is very simple.

print(dArr.T) #transpose

The output is:

[[3 7 8]

[5 5 9]

[7 3 1]]

In many situations, you will have to sum of elements present in an array.

#sum all elements in an array

print(np.sum(dArr))

#sum all elements in the rows or columns

print(np.sum(dArr, axis=0)) #0 axis means elements in rows, 1 means columns

print(np.sum(dArr, axis=1))

The outputs are:

48

[18 19 11]

[15 15 18]

Numpy library offers many more methods that can be applied to arrays. You are encouraged to explore all the available methods by experimenting with random arrays, it will help when dealing with practical tasks.

Matplotlib

When the data set is too large, it's difficult to understand what the data is telling you. Data visualization helps in this regard. You might not be able to detect a trend looking at thousands of numbers, but a simple line chart will instantly tell you what's the trend.

Let's create some charts using matplotlib library. But, first, we need to install this library in the virtual environment "tf" we created. In PyCharm, towards the bottom left side of your screen, you will see the "Terminal," switch to it. Run the command "activate tf". You will now see (tf) written before the command prompt. Now run "pip install matplotlib", and the external library will be downloaded and installed in our virtual environment.

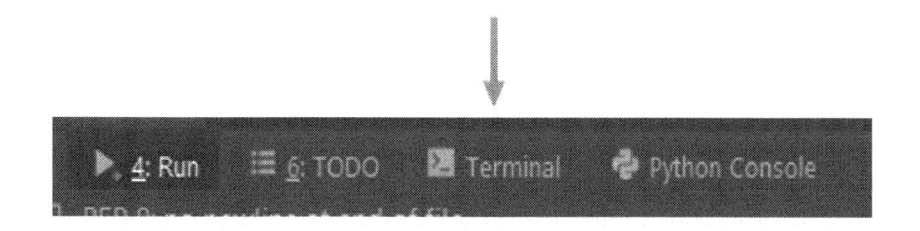

We can now start plotting charts. Here's an example of a simple line chart.

import matplotlib.pyplot as plt

import numpy as np

arr1 = np.array([2, 4, 6])

arr2 = np.array([3, 5, 7])

plt.plot(arr1, arr2)

plt.show()

The above script will output a straight line chart on the screen like this.

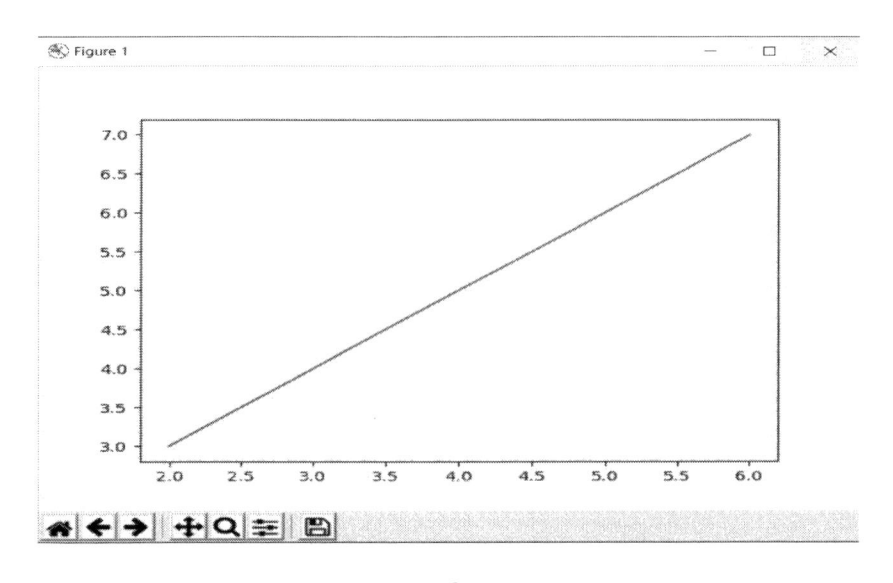

The plot has a few buttons on the bottom left side. You can reset the view with the "Home" button, cycle through different views using the "Arrow" buttons, move the plot around using the "Crosshair." The "Zoom" button will you let you zoom in (left click and drag) or out (right click and drag) of the plot view. The "Configuration" buttons gives you more options to change the plot view and looks like below. The last button, "Save," lets you save the plot as an image.

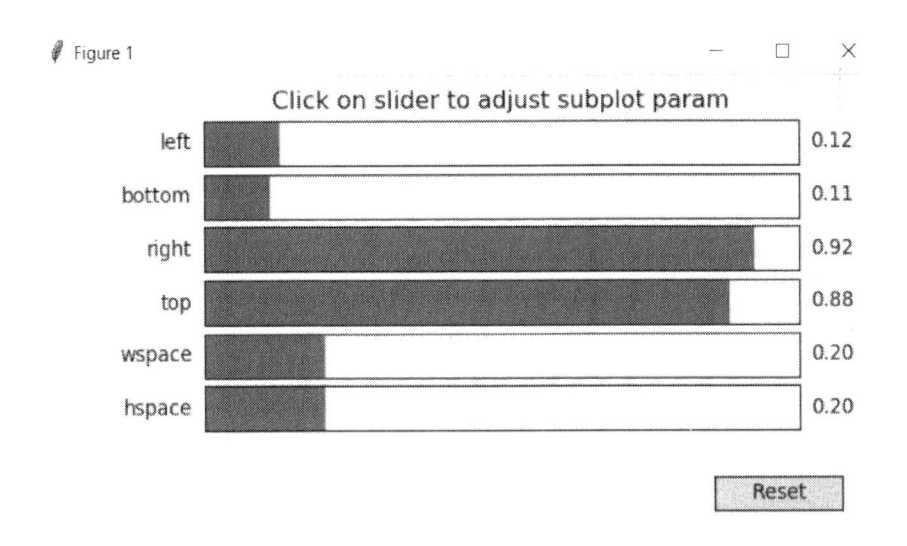

We can customize the plots by adding a title, labels, and a legend to our plot view. Here is the updated script.

import matplotlib.pyplot as plt

import numpy as np

arr1 = np.array([2, 4, 6])

```python
arr2 = np.array([3, 5, 7])


arr3 = np.array([-1, -3, -5])

arr4 = np.array([-2, -4, -6])


plt.plot(arr1, arr2, label="First Line")

plt.plot(arr3, arr4, label="Second Line")


plt.xlabel("X Axis")

plt.ylabel("Y Axis")

plt.title("Line Charts\nwith arbitrary values")


plt.legend()

plt.show()
```

The output now is:

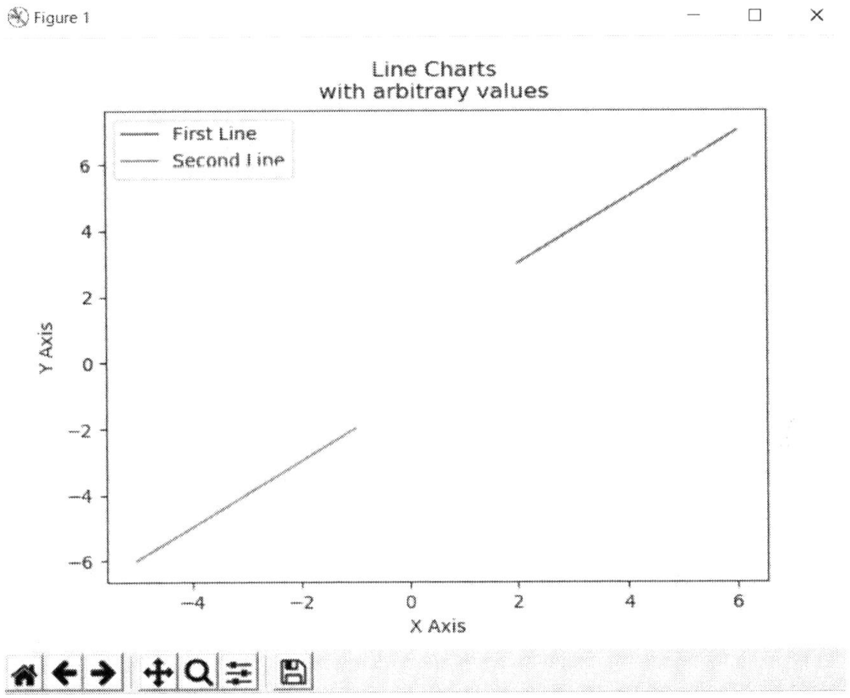
Figure 1
Line Charts
with arbitrary values
First Line
Second Line
Y Axis
X Axis
6
4
2
0
−2
−4
−6
−4
−2
0
2
4
6

Next, let's work with bar charts and histograms. Many people think both are the same, but our example will show how they differ. Here's an example of bar charts.

```
import matplotlib.pyplot as plt

import numpy as np



arr1 = np.array([2, 4, 6])

arr2 = np.array([3, 5, 7])
```

arr3 = np.array([3, 5, 7])

arr4 = np.array([12, 14, 16])

plt.bar(arr1, arr2, label="Bar Chart 1")

plt.bar(arr3, arr4, label="Bar Chart 2")

plt.title("Bar Chart\nwith arbitrary values")

plt.legend()

plt.show()

The output is:

Bar Chart with arbitrary values

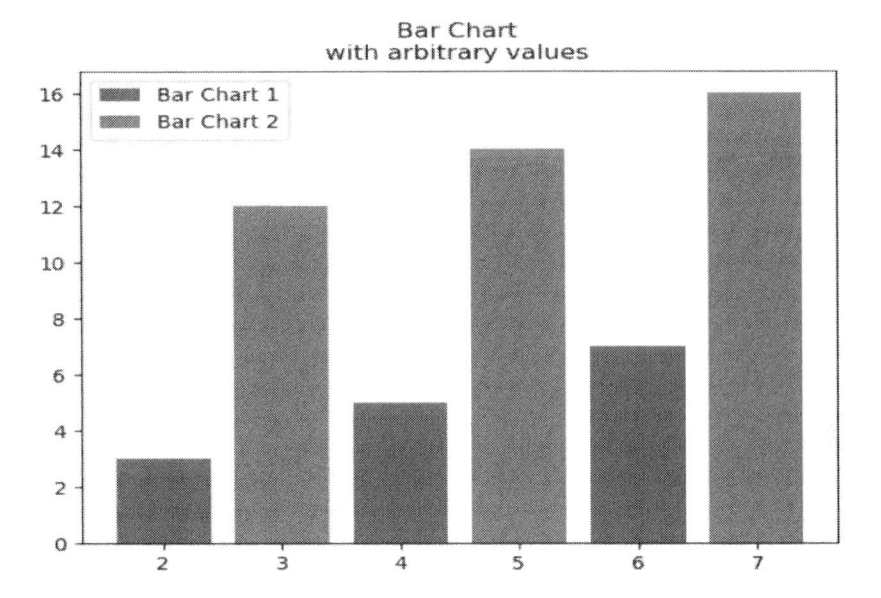

We can see that bar charts can be easily used to visually compare two different data sets.

A histogram is more often used to visualize the distribution of a data set over some specified period (usually time period). Here's a code to visualize the ages of a population sample in age groups of 10 years.

import matplotlib.pyplot as plt

import numpy as np

arr1 = np.array([16, 55, 21, 45, 85, 57, 32, 66, 94, 12, 25, 29, 30, 32, 45, 16, 12, 74, 63, 18]) rangeBin = [0, 10, 20, 30, 40, 50, 60, 70, 80, 90, 100]

plt.hist(arr1, rangeBin, histtype='bar', rwidth=0.9, label="Age Groups")

plt.title("Population Age Distribution")

plt.legend()

plt.show()

Here is the output chart.

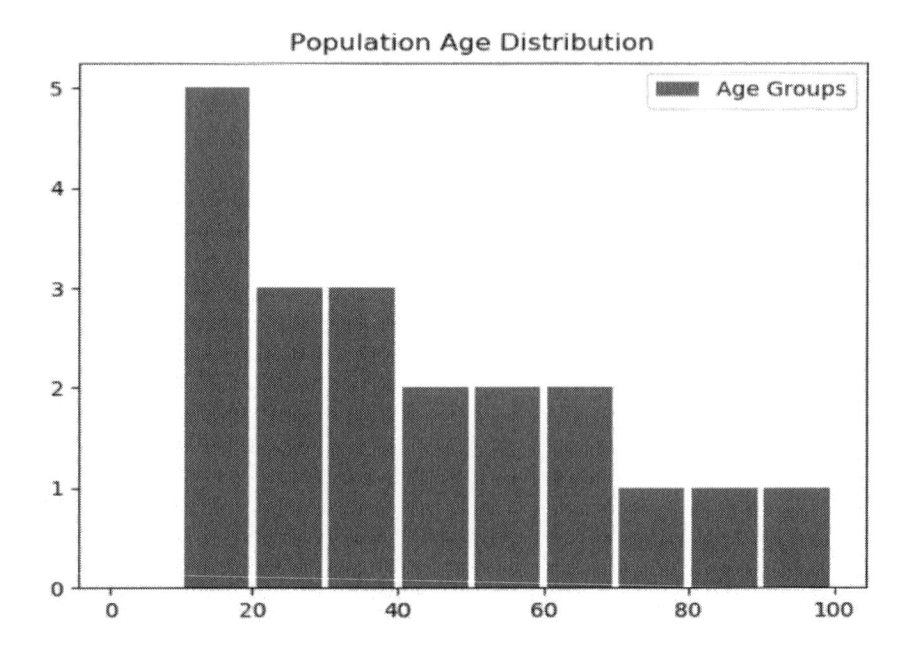

To change the bar colors, we add a "color" argument to the "plt.hist()" method.

plt.hist(arr1, rangeBin, histtype='bar', rwidth=0.9, label="Age Groups", color="teal")

The "rwidth" is set to 0.9 to separate the bars a little; otherwise, they would be plotted right next to each other forming a block.

Next up is scatter plot, which is usually used to show the relation between two variables.

import matplotlib.pyplot as plt

import numpy as np

arr1 = np.array([2, 4, 6, 7, 3, 7, 5])

arr2 = np.array([3, 5, 7, 2, 4, 7, 9])

plt.scatter(arr1, arr2, label="Scatter Data", color="teal", marker="*", s=1000)

plt.title("Scatter Plot")

plt.legend()

plt.show()

The output of the above script will be:

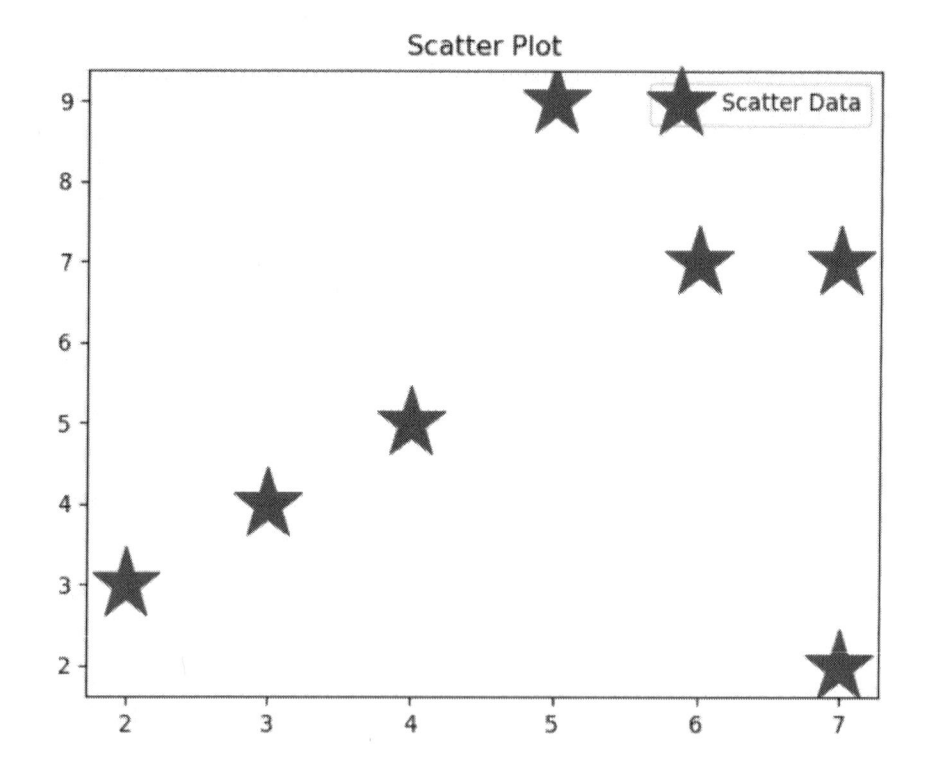

In a scatter plot, we can choose the marker type and size. Here, we have used a star, for a full list of available marker types, visit https://matplotlib.org/3.1.1/api/markers_api.html.

Another chart you can create with the Python matplotlib library is the stack plot which is used to show the contribution of several assets in achieving a certain point. It's much easier to understand if I show you an example.

```python
import matplotlib.pyplot as plt

import numpy as np


daysArr = np.array([1, 2, 3, 4, 5, 6, 7])


sleepArr = np.array([7, 8, 7.5, 8.25, 4, 9, 8])

eatArr = np.array([2, 1.5, 1.25, 0.5, 3, 4, 0.75])

workArr = np.array([8, 9, 7.5, 8.25, 7, 0.25, 0.5])

chillArr = np.array([7, 5.5, 7.75, 7, 10, 10.75, 14.75])


plt.stackplot(daysArr, sleepArr, eatArr, workArr, chillArr, labels=["Sleep", "Eat", "Work", "Chill"], colors=['m', 'c', 'r', 'k'])


plt.title("Stack Plot")

plt.legend()

plt.show()
```

The output is:

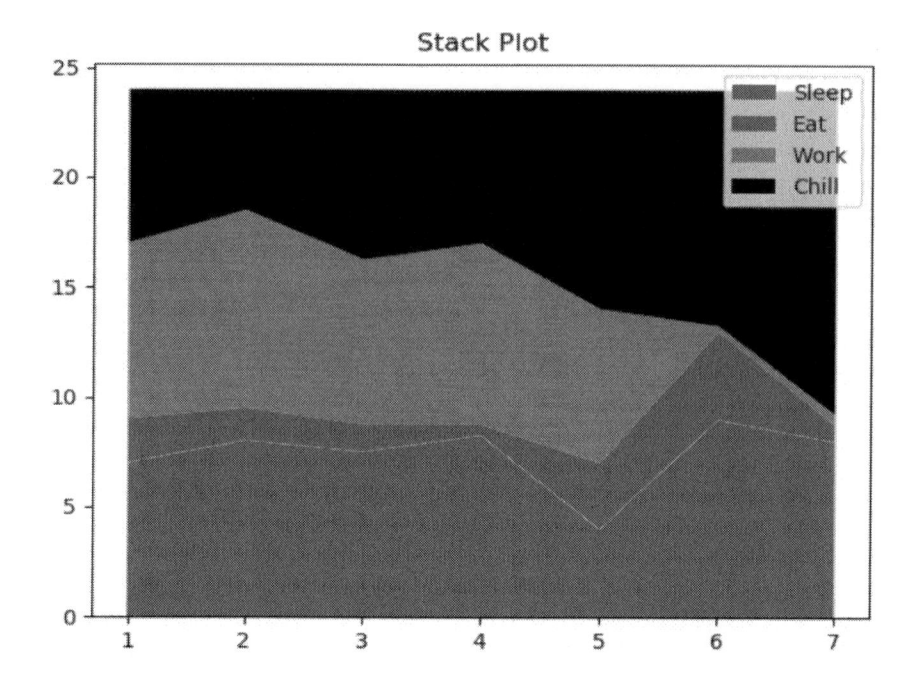

[Stack Plot figure]

We have used color codes for the stack plot, 'm' for magenta, 'c' for cyan, 'r' for red, and 'k' for black.

Let's move onto pie charts. Here's our activities example using a pie chart.

import matplotlib.pyplot as plt

import numpy as np

daysArr = np.array([1, 2, 3, 4, 5, 6, 7])

sleepArr = np.array([7, 8, 7.5, 8.25, 4, 9, 8])

eatArr = np.array([2, 1.5, 1.25, 0.5, 3, 4, 0.75])

workArr = np.array([8, 9, 7.5, 8.25, 7, 0.25, 0.5])

chillArr = np.array([7, 5.5, 7.75, 7, 10, 10.75, 14.75])

slices = np.array([8, 0.75, 0.5, 14.75]) #taking last values of all activity arrays to create an array detailing time spent on Sunday in different activities

plt.pie(slices, labels=["Sleep", "Eat", "Work", "Chill"], colors=['lightblue', 'r', 'm', 'teal'], explode=(0, 0.15, 0, 0), autopct="%1.1f%%")

plt.title("Pie Chart\nSunday activities")

plt.show()

The output is:

Pie Chart
Sunday activities

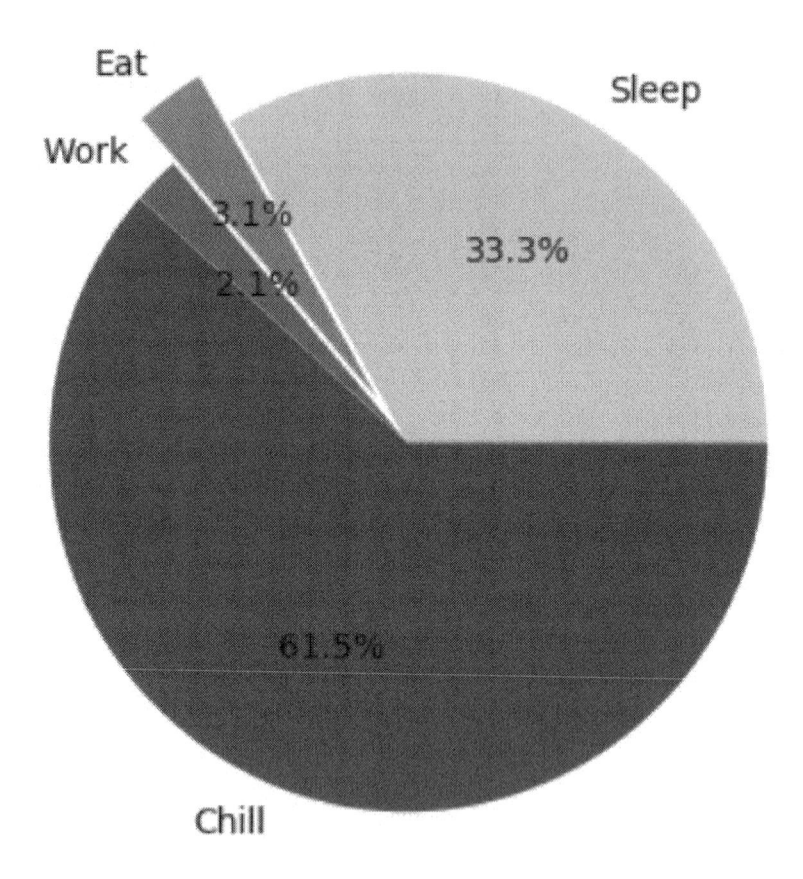

- Eat: 3.1%
- Work: 2.1%
- Sleep: 33.3%
- Chill: 61.5%

Pretty chill Sunday! Pie charts are a great way of showing how different things add up to complete the whole picture. We have used "explode" argument to make "Eating" stand out from the rest. The "autopct" argument can take special formatting to show the percentage each activity takes up the hours of my typical Sunday.

Data Acquisition

Up till now, we have declared random arrays to showcase different features of numpy and matplotlib libraries. In real-life tasks, you will need to access data from a certain source. The data set might be in a comma separated values (.csv) file which is sometimes also saved as a simple text (.txt) file, or maybe in another format like an excel (.xslx) file or maybe in XML or JSON format. Also, the source file might be located on your computer or on the internet.

How to acquire data in such cases? Let's look at a few examples.

Get data from local text file

Navigate to your PyCharm project directory (you can see the link of project folder besides the project name in Project pane of PyCharm) and create a file "example.txt". Add the following sample data to it, save and close the file.

1,45

2,23

3,12

4,54

5,74

6,21

7,5

8,68

9,24

10,8

There are many libraries that can be used to import data from a text/csv file. We are going to show two approaches, using the standard csv library and then the numpy library.

Here's the script using standard csv library to read data and plot the data using matplotlib.

import csv

import matplotlib.pyplot as plt

x = []

y = []

file = open('example.txt', 'r')

file_data = csv.reader(file, delimiter=",")

```
for row in file_data:

    x.append(int(row[0]))

    y.append(int(row[1]))


plt.plot(x, y)


plt.show()

file.close()
```

The output is:

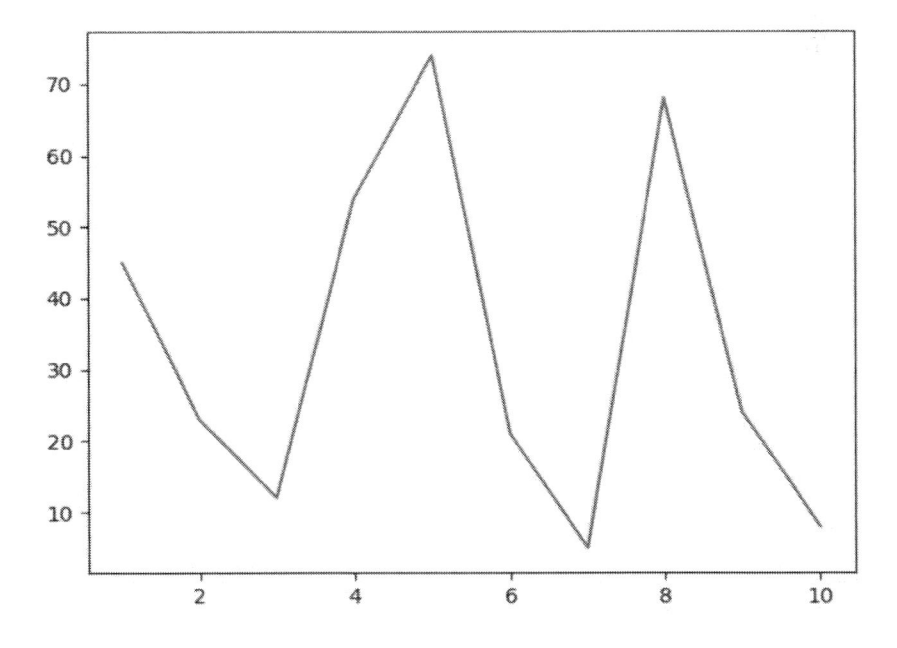

Let's use numpy to get the same result.

```
import numpy as np

import matplotlib.pyplot as plt


x, y = np.loadtxt('example.txt', delimiter=',', unpack=True)


plt.plot(x, y)


plt.show()
```

The output is the same. Yes, it's that simple with numpy! On top of that, it's faster. The "unpack" argument tells numpy to map the read data to the given variables.

Get data from internet

Most data accumulators provide APIs to enable programmers to communicate with their data. We are going to connect with Quandl using their API to download stock prices of certain companies and see the price trend.

Our code will be divided into three parts (each part will be a separate function).

1. The first part will acquire data through the API.

2. The second part will preprocess data so it's ready for plotting.
3. The third and final part will plot the data as a line chart.

Here is the complete code.

```python
import matplotlib.pyplot as plt

import urllib.request

from dateutil.parser import parse


api_key = "xxxxxxxxxxxxxxxxxx" #replace xxxxxxxxxxxxxxxxxx with your API key


def get_data(comp):

    stockPriceURL = "https://www.quandl.com/api/v3/datasets/WIKI/"+comp+".csv?api_key="+api_key

    getsource = urllib.request.urlopen(stockPriceURL).read().decode()

    return getsource


def filter_data(rawData):
```

```
        stockDate = []

        stockClose = []

        dataSplit = rawData.split('\n')

        for row in dataSplit[1:]:

            if row != "":

                elems = row.split(',')

                stockDate.append(parse(elems[0]))

                stockClose.append(float(elems[4]))

        return stockDate, stockClose


def plot_data(final_data):

    plt.plot(final_data[0], final_data[1])



    plt.xlabel("Year")

    plt.ylabel("Closing Stock Price")

    plt.title("Closing Stock Price Trend for TESLA (TSLA)\nfor the last ten yrs")
```

```
        plt.show()



def main():

        #company = input("Enter the company symbol you want to see price trend of: ") #enable this if user input is required

        company = "TSLA"

        rawData = get_data(company)

        final_data = filter_data(rawData)

        plot_data(final_data)



if __name__ == "__main__":

        main()
```

The output chart will be like this.

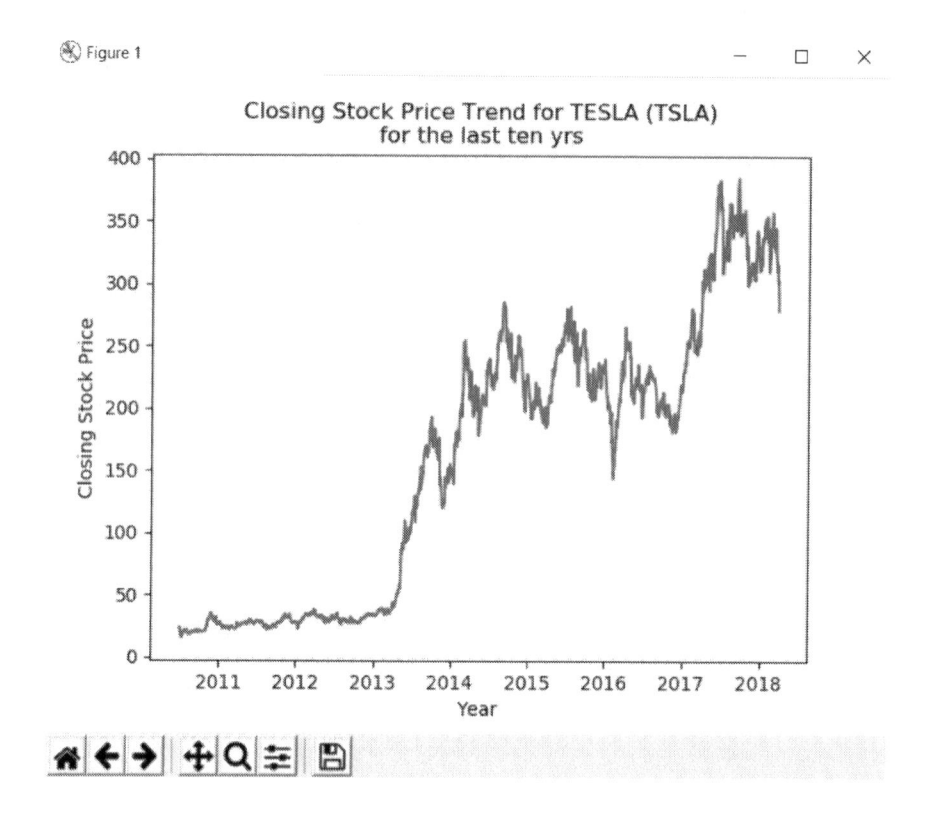

[Figure: Closing Stock Price Trend for TESLA (TSLA) for the last ten yrs, showing closing stock price from 2011 to 2018, ranging from near 0 to about 400]

Let's talk a bit about our code.

To use this code, we will have to first sign up with Quandl to use their API. The sign up is completely free, so complete it by going to this link:

https://www.quandl.com/sign-up-modal?defaultModal=showSignUp
and activate the account. You will be assigned an API key that you can place in the above code to use Quandl API services.

118

The data provided by Quandl has a header row. We have ignored the header row by slicing the list containing the parsed data (dataSplit[1:]). In the above script, I have focused on gathering dates (elems[0]) and the respective closing price (elems[4]) to plot the chart. The data from the .csv file is read as strings. We have to convert it to the correct format (date and floating) before trying to plot them using matplotlib. The date conversion is done through parse of the standard dateutil.parser library. The conversion of closing prices from string to floating is straightforward.

Another thing to note in the script is how we have returned two lists (stockDate and stockClose) in the function filter_data() and is gathered by the single list final_data, which results in concatenation of returned lists.

This is not the only way to acquire data from Quandl. We could have used numpy arrays instead of lists in our code that would have made things a little faster. Quandl also offers a special library for Python "quandl" that you can install using pip and use to access data from Quandl.

Let's setup quandl library on Python and see how we can perform the actions of the last script using the new library. Switch to "terminal" in PyCharm. Activate the "tf" virtual environment if not already active, and then use the following command to install quandl.

pip install quandl

Here is the code to display closing price trend for Apple (AAPL).

```python
import numpy as np

import matplotlib.pyplot as plt

import quandl


api_key = "xxxxxxxxxxxxxxxxxx" #replace xxxxxxxxxxxxxxxxxx with your API key


def get_data(comp):

    getsource = quandl.get("EOD/"+comp+".4", returns="numpy", authtoken=api_key, start_date="2009-01-01", end_date="2019-01-01")

    return getsource


def filter_data(rawData):

    dates = np.array([i[0] for i in rawData])

    closep = np.array([i[1] for i in rawData])
```

```python
    return dates, closep


def plot_data(final_data):

    #plt.plot(final_data[0], final_data[1], label="Price")

    plt.plot_date(final_data[0], final_data[1], '-', label="Price", color="gold")

    plt.xlabel("Half-Year")

    plt.ylabel("Closing Stock Price")

    plt.xticks(rotation=20)

    plt.title("Closing Stock Price Trend for APPLE (AAPL)\nusing all available data")

    plt.subplots_adjust(bottom=0.15)


    plt.legend()

    plt.show()


def main():
```

```
#company = input("Enter the company symbol you want to see price trend of: ") #enable this if user input is required

company = "AAPL"

rawData = get_data(company)

final_data = filter_data(rawData)

plot_data(final_data)


if __name__ == "__main__":

    main()
```

The above will output the following chart.

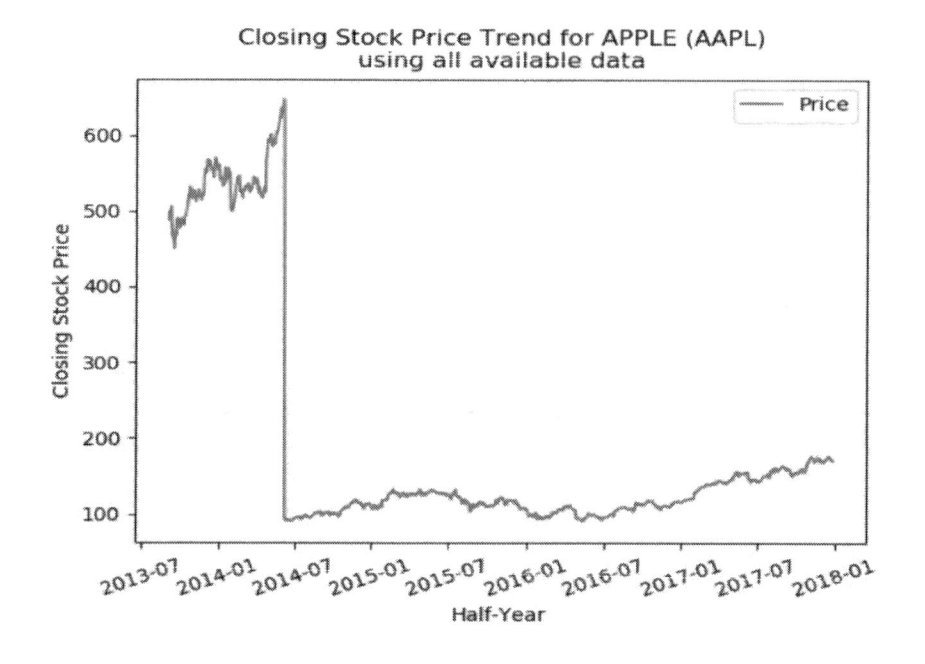

We can see from the trend that in mid-2014, the stock prices crashed for Apple. But, this wasn't because the company went out of business, Apple introduced split shares which allowed cheaper shares opening doors to micro investors. Other than that, Apple's stock price has a very distinctly repetitive trend. Any experienced stock trader can look at this trend and find opportunities of investing at the right time and making profits.

Let's talk about our script. TSLA stocks are not available on the free Quandl account so we will work with the available data of AAPL stocks. Quandly offers a lot of stock data, but we are only interested in the End of Day closing stock price, which is the fifth column of the Quandl data. In the get_data() function, we import the stock data as a numpy recarray. Numpy recarrays are different than normal numpy arrays because they can contain different data types wrapped in a tuple. The start and end dates are used to set a range for data, but in our example, both are useless because we have very limited set of data available on our free Quandl account.

We actually don't need to filter_data() function because the data is ready for plotting. For the sake of showing a new technique, we have used this function to create standard numpy arrays from the recarray Quandl generated. The function returns both arrays and collected as a tuple by the main() function. Note that this is not a good practice as we are dealing with a huge data set. Can you think of a better way to pass data from filter_data() to main()?

In the plot_data() function, we have shown two different plotting methods, one we already know plt.plot() and the other plt.plot_date(). The plot_date() is very useful in plotting two quantities in which one is time. We have also used some advanced plot formatting to make the plot look nicer. The labels on the 'x' axis are rotated to avoid overlap and the plot margin from the bottom is increased so nothing overflows out of the visible window. One more thing, plot_date() usually plots a scatter plot instead of a line chart, we have added the '-' argument to force plot_date() in creating a line chart.

You might see the following warning because we didn't explicitly set the data format conversion. But, we can ignore this warning because our script is correctly plotting the data.

To register the converters:

>>> from pandas.plotting import register_matplotlib_converters

>>> register_matplotlib_converters()

warnings.warn(msg, FutureWarning)

The quandl library is a very powerful tool if you want to write scripts on stocks and other finance applications. The free account has some API call limitations, but you can download the entire data set of any symbol (company traded in a stock market) using the API URL method to your computer and then keep practicing different analysis and machine-learning techniques with the offline data set.

A project

We have learned enough to consider a real-world scenario and attempt to solve the issue(s) using the tools we have learned so far. Here's a scenario.

We have been contracted by a potato chips manufacturing facility that makes 200g packets. We have to find if a randomly picked chips packet from the assembly line has a net weight within the accepted tolerance range of ±10g. We ask the facility to sample a random number of samples and record the mean weight and standard deviation. The values come up as 197.9g and 5.5g respectively.

We start by assuming the system probability has a normal distribution. We have a complex and randomly sampled system so it's impossible to ascertain the probability of a specific event through the normal probability determination methods. To find the probability of such as a complex system, we create the probability distribution curve and find area under the curve.

In our code, we have used a library we haven't used so far, the "scipy" library. The erf() from math library is used to estimate the error function of a normal distribution system. We are also using the subplot().

Import required libraries

```python
from math import erf, sqrt

import numpy as np

import matplotlib.pyplot as plt

from scipy.stats import norm


# Declare given data

sysAvg = 197.9

sysDevStd = 5.5

sysLowTol = 190

sysHighTol = 210


''' Calculating probability '''

# Probability from Z=0 to lower bound

lowTolProb = erf((sysLowTol - sysAvg) / (sysDevStd * sqrt(2))) / 2


# Probability from Z=0 to upper bound
```

highTolProb = erf((sysHighTol - sysAvg) / (sysDevStd * sqrt(2))) / 2

Calculate Interval Probabilities

pIn = highTolProb - lowTolProb

pOut = 1 - pIn

Print data and results

print('===Given Data===')

print('Mean = %.1fg \nStandard Deviation: %.1fg' % (sysAvg, sysDevStd))

print('Tolerance range = %.1fg <--> %.1fg \n' % (sysLowTol, sysHighTol))

print('===Calculation Results===')

print('Lower Bound = %.4f' % lowTolProb)

print('Upper Bound = %.4f' % highTolProb)

print('Probability of finding a chips packet with weight within the tolerance range (pIn) = %.1f%%' % (pIn*100)) # using %% to print a percent symbol

```
print('Probability of finding a chips packet with weight outside the tolerance range (pOut) = %.1f%% \n' % (pOut*100)) # using %% to print a percent symbol
```

```
''' Plotting distribution curve '''

# Calculate the Z-scores

z1 = (sysLowTol - sysAvg) / sysDevStd

z2 = (sysHighTol - sysAvg) / sysDevStd


# Calculate the plot values

x = np.arange(z1, z2, 0.001)  # range of x-axis within tolerance range

x_all = np.arange(-4, 4, 0.001)  # entire range of x-axis, both in and out of tolerance range

# mean = 0, sysDevStd = 1, since Z-scores were calculated, norm.pdf calculates the probability density function

y = norm.pdf(x, 0, 1)

y_all = norm.pdf(x_all, 0, 1)
```

Build the plot

fig, ax = plt.subplots(figsize=(12, 9)) # set plot height and width

plt.style.use('fivethirtyeight') # set color scheme

ax.plot(x_all, y_all, label="Probability Range") # setting label here is necessary, otherwise plt.legend() would throw an error

Add custom styling to the plot

ax.fill_between(x, y, 0, alpha=0.3, color='yellow') # alpha argument is used to create a shade of yellow color

ax.fill_between(x_all, y_all, 0, alpha=0.1, color='red') # alpha argument is used to create a shade of red color

ax.set_xlabel('Standardized Mean')

ax.set_ylabel('Probability Density')

ax.set_title('System Distribution Curve')

Show the plot

plt.legend()

plt.savefig('sysProbCurve.png')   # Save the plot in current working directory, this must be done before plot.show() or you might end up with a blank image file

plt.show()

We are also saving the plot as a "png" image in the current working file. As stated in the comment, we have to save the file before showing it on the screen or we might end up with a blank image. In our plot, we have used shading to highlight areas of interest. Yellow color shows the area of probability to find a chips packet with weight within the tolerance range, which is more than the area with red color, which shows the probability of picking a packet outside the range.

The output of the above code is below.

===Given Data===

Mean = 197.9g

Standard Deviation: 5.5g

Tolerance range = 190.0g <--> 210.0g

===Calculation Results===

Lower Bound = -0.4246

Upper Bound = 0.4861

Probability of finding a chips packet with weight within the tolerance range (pIn) = 91.1%

Probability of finding a chips packet with weight outside the tolerance range (pOut) = 8.9%

There is a 91.1% chance of picking a chips packet from the production line and its weight being within the tolerance range. Is it a high enough percentage? It depends upon the production facility and the standards it has to keep up with. Note that there are industrial standards and government inspections to make sure the final product follows the claims made. The weight of the packet is one such important parameter.

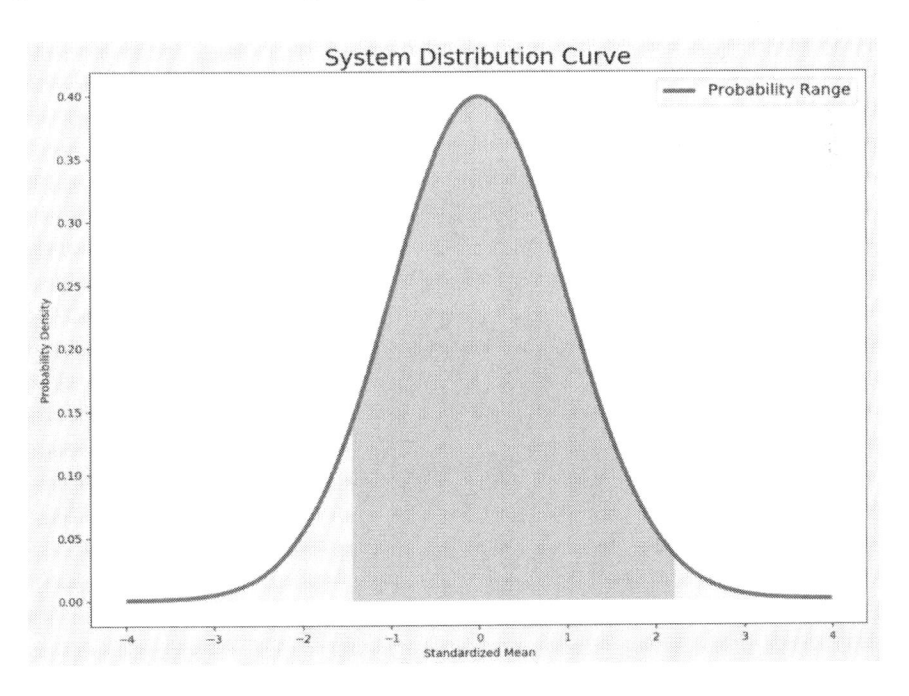

The Pandas Framework

"Pandas" framework provides even more flexibility and options when dealing with large data sets. It is the most versatile data structure available, and you can handle almost all data-related work with pandas. It is also better than other data processing options; for example, if you are still thinking of using a spreadsheet software to perform data analysis, you are missing on a much faster option. One more fact, using pandas and numpy using Python to perform data analysis and machine learning is as fast as using another language like C++ because these libraries are based on the C language with a Python wrapper. So, we have faster processing of C family languages and the easy syntax of Python greatly enhancing coding experience and results.

The pandas framework also makes it easier to read data from any data source. No matter the source, the data read has always the same format which makes it easier for the scriptwriter to handle it.

To facilitate dealing with massive data sets, the pandas framework offers two data structures, series and data frames. Let's discuss the basics of both.

Series

What happens when the best features of dictionaries and numpy arrays are combined together? The pandas framework "series" data structure is the result. Let's do some basic work with pandas series.

from pandas import Series

import pandas as pd

aSer = Series([2, 4, 6])

print(aSer)

print(aSer.values) # get all values as a list

print(aSer.index) # get all indices as a list

keys = ['frst', 'scnd', 'thrd']

bSer = Series([3, 5, 7], index=keys)

print(bSer)

print(bSer['frst']) # get element using key

print(bSer[0]) # get element using index

```
aDict = {

    'a': 1,

    'b': 2,

    'c': 0

}

cSer = Series(aDict)  # creating a series from a dictionary


print(cSer)


ind = ['a', 'b', 'd']

dSer = Series(aDict, index=ind)  # if key isn't in the dictionary, "NaN" is added as value to that key


print(dSer)


print(pd.isnull(dSer['d']))  # check if an element has "NaN" value
```

dSer.name = 'Data'

dSer.index.name = 'Index'

print(dSer)

dSer.index = ['un', 'deux', 'nul']   # keys are mutable unlike standard dictionaries

print(dSer)

The outputs of the above "print" statements are:

0   2

1   4

2   6

dtype: int64

[2 4 6]

RangeIndex(start=0, stop=3, step=1)

frst   3

scnd   5

thrd   7

dtype: int64

3

3

a   1

b   2

c   0

dtype: int64

a   1.0

b   2.0

d   NaN

dtype: float64

True

Index

a   1.0

b   2.0

d   NaN

Name: Data, dtype: float64

un   1.0

deux   2.0

nul   NaN

Name: Data, dtype: float64

Time Series

Any quantity that can be measured for a period of time forms a time series. This series is very important in different fields including finance, economics, ecology, neuroscience, and physics. The quantity might be sampled after fixed intervals (fixed frequency) or sampled at random times (irregular). We are going to take a look at the following time series.

1. Timestamps – quantity sampled at specific time instants.
2. Fixed periods – quantity sampled after a fixed time period, like monthly, annually, etc.
3. Intervals – quantity sampled for a range of time.

Timestamps are the most common and simplest time series.

The pandas framework provides access to various tools and algorithms to work with large time series. You can easily resample, aggregate, and segment a time series. The available resources are very useful in various applications such as analyzing log files.

from datetime import datetime

from datetime import timedelta

from dateutil.parser import parse

now = datetime.now()

print(now)   # the returned data has year, month, day, hour, minutes, seconds, milliseconds, and microseconds

nexTime = now + timedelta(12)   # 12 means the nexTime will be 12 days in advance from now

print(nexTime)

print(str(nexTime))   # string looks the same as datatime format print(nexTime.strftime('%Y-%m-%d'))   # reformat datetime value

ranTime = '1990-03-07'

print(datetime.strptime(ranTime, '%Y-%m-%d'))   # format string as datetime

print(parse(ranTime)) # format string that has datetime format as datetime without specifying a format

print(parse(ranTime, dayfirst=True))   # put the day before month to follow international locales

The respective outputs of the above print statements are:

2019-10-30 08:10:25.841218

2019-11-11 08:10:25.841218

2019-11-11 08:10:25.841218

2019-11-11

1990-03-07 00:00:00

1990-03-07 00:00:00

1990-07-03 00:00:00

In a time series, we deal with a set of time values usually used as a column or axis index in a dataframe. We can create indexes using a list containing strings that have date related data.

stringDates = ['1958-01-31', '1969-07-20']

print(pd.to_datetime(stringDates))   # converts an array of strings that look like used as index for a dataframe

print(pd.to_datetime(stringDates + [None]))   # we can use "none" as an index which translates to NaT (Not a Time)

The outputs are:

DatetimeIndex(['1958-01-31', '1969-07-20'], dtype='datetime64[ns]', freq=None)

DatetimeIndex(['1958-01-31', '1969-07-20', 'NaT'], dtype='datetime64[ns]', freq=None)

Once we have the time indices, we can create a pandas series or dataframe resulting in a time series. Here's an example of a time series using series.

stringDates = ['1958-01-31', '1969-07-20']

print(pd.to_datetime(stringDates))   # converts an array of strings that look like used as index for a dataframe

dateIndices = pd.to_datetime(stringDates + [None])

print(dateIndices)   # we can use "none" as an index which translates to NaT (Not a Time)

tSer = Series(np.random.randn(2), index=pd.to_datetime(stringDates))

tSer2 = Series(np.random.randn(3), index=dateIndices)

print(tSer)

print(tSer2)

print(tSer + tSer2) # performing arithmetic operations on time series is easy

print(tSer * tSer2) # notice how NaT becomes the first element

The outputs are:

DatetimeIndex(['1958-01-31', '1969-07-20'], dtype='datetime64[ns]', freq=None)

DatetimeIndex(['1958-01-31', '1969-07-20', 'NaT'], dtype='datetime64[ns]', freq=None)

1958-01-31   2.520516

1969-07-20   0.305652

dtype: float64

1958-01-31   -0.720893

1969-07-20   1.213476

NaT   -0.229652

dtype: float64

NaT   NaN

1958-01-31   1.799623

1969-07-20   1.519128

dtype: float64

NaT   NaN

1958-01-31 -1.817023

1969-07-20   0.370901

dtype: float64

We can also perform index slicing on a time series. Time series can also contain duplicate indices. Here's a script that showcases bot concepts.

longtSer = Series(np.random.randn(500), index=pd.date_range('7/3/2016', periods=500)) # create a long time series and populate with random numbers

print(longtSer.head()) # get first five rows

print(longtSer[:5]) # use index slicing to get the same result: first five rows

print(longtSer['2016-07']) # we can slice the data using the month or year or even the day

print(longtSer.tail()) # get last five rows

print(longtSer[-5:]) # use negative index slicing to get the same result: last five rows

```
dates = pd.DatetimeIndex(['1/1/2019', '1/1/2019', '1/2/2019', '1/2/2019', '1/3/2019'])

duplSer = Series(np.arange(5), index=dates)  # time series can have duplicate indices

print(duplSer)

print(duplSer.index.is_unique)   # check if there are any duplicate time indices

grupdSer = duplSer.groupby(level=0)  # create a group object where values with same indices are grouped together

print(grupdSer.mean())  # get mean of grouped values for each duplicate time index

print(grupdSer.count())  # get count of grouped values for each duplicate time index
```

The outputs are:

2016-07-03   2.008307

2016-07-04   0.953226

2016-07-05 -0.355272

2016-07-06 -1.002089

2016-07-07 -1.609062

Freq: D, dtype: float64

2016-07-03   2.008307

2016-07-04   0.953226

2016-07-05 -0.355272

2016-07-06 -1.002089

2016-07-07 -1.609062

Freq: D, dtype: float64

2016-07-03   2.008307

2016-07-04   0.953226

2016-07-05 -0.355272

2016-07-06 -1.002089

2016-07-07 -1.609062

2016-07-08 -0.383618

2016-07-09 -0.346427

2016-07-10   0.449504

2016-07-11   0.099086

2016-07-12   0.311142

2016-07-13   -1.197215

2016-07-14   -1.014129

2016-07-15   -0.260970

2016-07-16   1.270730

2016-07-17   1.118838

2016-07-18   -0.461846

2016-07-19   -0.152710

2016-07-20   1.274209

2016-07-21   -0.175187

2016-07-22   -0.724205

2016-07-23   0.278828

2016-07-24   0.413432

2016-07-25   1.234999

2016-07-26   -0.425415

2016-07-27   -1.788413

2016-07-28   3.147094

2016-07-29   0.216745

2016-07-30   -0.674562

2016-07-31   -1.958297

Freq: D, dtype: float64

2017-11-10   0.319045

2017-11-11   0.614589

2017-11-12   0.479498

2017-11-13   -0.287627

2017-11-14   -1.362115

Freq: D, dtype: float64

2017-11-10   0.319045

2017-11-11   0.614589

2017-11-12   0.479498

2017-11-13   -0.287627

2017-11-14   -1.362115

Freq: D, dtype: float64

2019-01-01   0

2019-01-01   1

2019-01-02   2

2019-01-02   3

2019-01-03   4

dtype: int32

False

2019-01-01   0.5

2019-01-02   2.5

2019-01-03   4.0

dtype: float64

2019-01-01   2

2019-01-02   2

2019-01-03   1

dtype: int64

Dataframes

The second data structure offered by pandas is the dataframes. It's very fast and can handle gigabytes of data, which makes dataframes the best choice to use in machine learning.

Let's see a few basic dataframe operations.

import pandas as pd

dayLst = ['Mon', 'Tue', 'Wed', 'Thur', 'Fri', 'Sat', 'Sun']

siteStats = {

    "Day Number": [1, 2, 3, 4, 5, 6, 7],

    "Visitors": [1405, 24517, 32415, 74512, 9541, 32145, 33],

    "Bounce Rate": [65, 42, 54, 74, 82, 10, 35]

}

dFrame = pd.DataFrame(siteStats, index=dayLst) # using a list to assign custom indices to the dataframe

dFrame2 = pd.DataFrame(siteStats)

```python
dFrame2.set_index('Day Number', inplace=True)  # assigning existing dataframe column as the index


print(dFrame)

print(dFrame2)
```

The output is:

	Day Number	Visitors	Bounce Rate
Mon	1	1405	65
Tue	2	24517	42
Wed	3	32415	54
Thur	4	74512	74
Fri	5	9541	82
Sat	6	32145	10
Sun	7	33	35

	Visitors	Bounce Rate
Day Number		
1	1405	65

2	24517	42
3	32415	54
4	74512	74
5	9541	82
6	32145	10
7	33	35

One important thing to remember with pandas dataframe is that when you apply any methods such as set_index(), you get a new dataframe and the original dataframe remains intact. This is a safety feature so you don't accidentally overwrite the source data. If you want to overwrite the original data set, you have to use the "inplace=True" argument.

We can access a specific column or columns of a dataframe. We can also convert those columns to a numpy array, which leads to a question: can we convert a numpy array to a dataframe? Yes, we can. Here's a script that does all that.

print(dFrame['Bounce_Rate'])   # returns a single column of dataframe as a series with the same index as the dataframe

print(dFrame.Bounce_Rate)   # only works if column headers don't have spaces, returns the same output as above print

print(dFrame[['Visitors', 'Bounce_Rate']])   # returns multiple columns of dataframe as new dataframe with same index as the original

print(np.array(dFrame[['Visitors', 'Bounce_Rate']]))   # returns multiple columns of dataframe as multidim numpy array

dFrame3 = np.array(dFrame[['Visitors', 'Bounce_Rate']])   # convert a numpy array to a pandas dataframe

print(dFrame3)

The output of the above script is:

Mon   65

Tue   42

Wed   54

Thur   74

Fri   82

Sat   10

Sun   35

Name: Bounce_Rate, dtype: int64

Mon   65

Tue   42

Wed   54

Thur   74

Fri   82

Sat   10

Sun   35

Name: Bounce_Rate, dtype: int64

	Visitors	Bounce_Rate
Mon	1405	65
Tue	24517	42
Wed	32415	54
Thur	74512	74
Fri	9541	82
Sat	32145	10
Sun	33	35

```
[[ 1405      65]

[24517    42]

[32415    54]

[74512    74]

[ 9541    82]

[32145    10]

[   33    35]]
```

As the output suggests, when we access a single column of a dataframe by using the column header and we get a list. In our script, we created a dataframe from a dictionary. The dictionary keys were set without spaces that makes each column a parameter of the dataframe.

Reading Data

The pandas framework also provides out of the box support to get data from most common data set file formats from both local or external sources. We have already learned how to connect with Quandl using it's API URL or the quandl Python library to access data. What if the data is already downloaded from Quandl and currently residing on your computer? We can also read data from there. Login to your Quandl account by going to their website. Search for "AAPL", which is the stock price data for Apple Inc. Quandl provides data export feature in many file formats. Let's download in the .csv format to the current PyCharm project folder.

```python
import pandas as pd

''' # getting data from a CSV file on local computer'''

dataF = pd.read_csv('EOD-AAPL.csv')


dataF.set_index('Date', inplace=True)  # set date as the index making this a time series dataframe

dataF.to_csv("new.csv")  # save dataframe data in a new csv file


print(dataF.head())


dataF = pd.read_csv('new.csv', index_col=0)  # if we want to read csv data and set the index at the same time, this is how it's done


print(dataF.head())
```

dataF.rename(columns={'Open': 'Open_Price'}, inplace=True) # renamed a column, we can rename multiple columns by passing more key-values in the columns dictionary

print(dataF.head())

dataF.to_csv("new2.csv", header=False) # save dataframe data in a new csv file without the headers

dataF = pd.read_csv('new2.csv', names=['Date', 'Open', 'High', 'Low', 'Close', 'Volume', 'Dividend', 'Split', 'Adj_Open', 'Adj_High', 'Adj_Low', 'Adj_Close', 'Adj_Volume'], index_col=0) # setting column headers if csv file doesn't have headers or if you want to rename columns

print(dataF.head())

The output of the above script is:

Date   Open   High   Low ...   Adj_Low   Adj_Close Adj_Volume

2017-12-28 171.00 171.850 170.480 ... 165.957609
166.541693 16480187.0

2017-12-27 170.10 170.780 169.710 ... 165.208036
166.074426 21498213.0

2017-12-26 170.80 171.470 169.679 ... 165.177858
166.045222 33185536.0

2017-12-22 174.68 175.424 174.500 ... 169.870969
170.367440 16349444.0

2017-12-21 174.17 176.020 174.100 ... 169.481580
170.367440 20949896.0

[5 rows x 12 columns]

Date   Open   High   Low ...   Adj_Low Adj_Close Adj_Volume

2017-12-28 171.00 171.850 170.480 ... 165.957609
166.541693 16480187.0

2017-12-27 170.10 170.780 169.710 ... 165.208036
166.074426 21498213.0

2017-12-26 170.80 171.470 169.679 ... 165.177858
166.045222 33185536.0

2017-12-22 174.68 175.424 174.500 ... 169.870969
170.367440 16349444.0

2017-12-21 174.17 176.020 174.100 ... 169.481580
170.367440 20949896.0

[5 rows x 12 columns]

Date   Open_Price High   Low ...   Adj_Low
Adj_Close Adj_Volume

2017-12-28   171.00 171.850 170.480 ... 165.957609
166.541693 16480187.0

2017-12-27   170.10 170.780 169.710 ... 165.208036
166.074426 21498213.0

2017-12-26   170.80 171.470 169.679 ... 165.177858
166.045222 33185536.0

2017-12-22   174.68 175.424 174.500 ... 169.870969
170.367440 16349444.0

2017-12-21 174.17 176.020 174.100 ... 169.481580
170.367440 20949896.0

[5 rows x 12 columns]

Date   Open High Low ... Adj_Low Adj_Close Adj_Volume

2017-12-28 171.00 171.850 170.480 ... 165.957609
166.541693 16480187.0

2017-12-27 170.10 170.780 169.710 ... 165.208036
166.074426 21498213.0

2017-12-26 170.80 171.470 169.679 ... 165.177858
166.045222 33185536.0

2017-12-22 174.68 175.424 174.500 ... 169.870969
170.367440 16349444.0

2017-12-21 174.17 176.020 174.100 ... 169.481580
170.367440 20949896.0

[5 rows x 12 columns]

As you can see, all the print statements have given identical outputs. That was the goal of the above script, to show different ways to read data from .csv files set with slightly different data form and to normalize them to one form.

Writing Data

Using the pandas framework, we can save dataframes in file formats other than we imported it from. For example, let's save our dataframe as an HTML file.

`dataF.to_html('dataF.html')  # save dataframe as an HTML file`

The new HTML file will be saved in the directory of current project. If you open the file using a browser, you will see the following.

Date	Open	High	Low	Close	Volume	Dividend	Split	Adj_Open	Adj_High	Adj_Low	Adj_Close	Adj_Volume
2017-12-28	171.0000	171.8500	170.4800	171.080000	16480187.0	0.00	1.0	166.463815	167.291267	165.957609	166.541693	16480187.0
2017-12-27	170.1000	170.7800	169.7100	170.600000	21498213.0	0.00	1.0	165.587690	166.249651	165.208036	166.074426	21498213.0
2017-12-26	170.8000	171.4700	169.6790	170.570000	33185536.0	0.00	1.0	166.269121	166.921347	165.177858	166.045222	33185536.0
2017-12-22	174.6800	175.4240	174.5000	175.010000	16349444.0	0.00	1.0	170.046194	170.770458	169.870969	170.367440	16349444.0
2017-12-21	174.1700	176.0200	174.1000	175.010000	20949896.0	0.00	1.0	169.549723	171.350648	169.481580	170.367440	20949896.0
2017-12-20	174.8700	175.4200	173.2500	174.350000	23475649.0	0.00	1.0	170.231154	170.766564	168.654129	169.724948	23475649.0
2017-12-19	175.0300	175.3900	174.0900	174.540000	27436447.0	0.00	1.0	170.386910	170.737360	169.471846	169.909908	27436447.0
2017-12-18	174.8800	177.2000	174.8600	176.420000	29421114.0	0.00	1.0	170.240889	172.499345	170.221419	171.740037	29421114.0
2017-12-15	173.6300	174.1700	172.4600	173.970000	40169307.0	0.00	1.0	169.024048	169.549723	167.885085	169.355029	40169307.0
2017-12-14	172.4000	173.1300	171.6500	172.220000	20476541.0	0.00	1.0	167.826677	168.537312	167.096572	167.651452	20476541.0
2017-12-13	172.5000	173.5400	172.0000	172.270000	23818447.0	0.00	1.0	167.924024	168.936436	167.437238	167.700125	23818447.0
2017-12-12	172.1500	172.3900	171.4610	171.700000	19409230.0	0.00	1.0	167.583309	167.816942	166.912586	167.145246	19409230.0
2017-12-11	169.2000	172.8900	168.7900	172.670000	35273759.0	0.00	1.0	164.711565	168.303678	164.312441	168.089514	35273759.0
2017-12-08	170.4900	171.0000	168.8200	169.370000	23355231.0	0.00	1.0	165.967344	166.463815	164.341645	164.877055	23355231.0
2017-12-07	169.0300	170.4400	168.9100	169.320000	25673308.0	0.00	1.0	164.546074	165.918671	164.429257	164.828381	25673308.0

If you open the same HTML file in a text editor, you will see the following.

`<table border="1" class="dataframe">`

`<thead>`

```
<tr style="text-align: right;">
    <th></th>
    <th>Open</th>
    <th>High</th>
    <th>Low</th>
    <th>Close</th>
    <th>Volume</th>
    <th>Dividend</th>
    <th>Split</th>
    <th>Adj_Open</th>
    <th>Adj_High</th>
    <th>Adj_Low</th>
    <th>Adj_Close</th>
    <th>Adj_Volume</th>
</tr>
...
```

Getting Data from Internet

Here is a code that gets stock price data of Google (GOOG) from Yahoo Finance site using the special pandas_datareader library. We have to first install this library using pip. Switch to Terminal in PyCharm and make sure "tf" environment is activated; if not, activate it with following command.

```
activate tf
```

Then run the pip command.

```
pip install pandas_datareader
```

Once installed, run the following script.

```python
import pandas_datareader.data as web

import matplotlib.pyplot as plt

from matplotlib import style


rangeStart = '1/1/2009'

rangeStop = '1/1/2019'


dFrame = web.get_data_yahoo('GOOG', rangeStart, rangeStop)
```

print(dFrame.head()) #output first five rows of the dataframe

style.use('ggplot')

dFrame['Adj Close'].plot()

plt.show()

The output will be:

Date	High	Low	...	Volume	Adj Close
2009-01-02	160.309128	152.179596	...	7248000.0	160.060059
2009-01-05	165.001541	156.911850	...	9814500.0	163.412491
2009-01-06	169.763687	162.585587	...	12898500.0	166.406265
2009-01-07	164.837143	158.779861	...	9022600.0	160.403763
2009-01-08	161.987823	158.077484	...	7228300.0	161.987823

[5 rows x 6 columns]

The plotted graph will look like the following. Note how it looks different than our previous charts because we used the preset style "ggplot".

Machine-Learning Projects

We have learned enough tools and procedures to start dealing with real-life scenarios. Let's do two projects that will show us how machine learning can be beneficial in solving problems.

Predicting If a Country's GDP is Related to Its Better Life Index

Remember when we talked about whether happiness and money are related? Let's write some script to find out the relationship between the two using data of a few countries.

```python
import matplotlib
import matplotlib.pyplot as plt
import numpy as np
import pandas as pd
import sklearn

# Load the data
oecd_bli = pd.read_csv("oecd_bli_2015.csv", thousands=',')
gdp_per_capita = pd.read_csv("gdp_per_capita.csv",thousands=',',delimiter='\t',
encoding='latin1', na_values="n/a")

# Prepare the data
country_stats = prepare_country_stats(oecd_bli, gdp_per_capita)
X = np.c_[country_stats["GDP per capita"]]
y = np.c_[country_stats["Life satisfaction"]]

# Visualize the data
country_stats.plot(kind='scatter', x="GDP per capita", y='Life satisfaction')
```

```
plt.show()

# Select a linear model

model = sklearn.linear_model.LinearRegression()

# Train the model

model.fit(X, y)

# Make a prediction for Cyprus

X_new = [[22587]] # Cyprus' GDP per capita

print(model.predict(X_new)) # outputs [[ 5.96242338]]
```

Predicting Real Estate Prices for Investment

A real estate tycoon Mr. Gill from New York wants to expand his investment portfolio and is actively considering making substantial investment in other states of the US. Luckily, a common acquaintance introduced you to him and he offered you a big paycheck contract. You have only job, to find if he should invest in real estate of a specific state right away, delay, or stop thinking about new investment ventures altogether?

The first step is to gather real estate pricing data for the area. We are going to use Quandl as the data source. After we have the data, we will find correlation of the Housing Price Index (HPI) of all the states with each other and the national HPI. We will plot all the information to visualize the HPI trends for the last 44 years.

```
import pandas as pd

import quandl

import matplotlib.pyplot as plt

from matplotlib import style


# HPI = Housing Price Index


api_key = "xxxxxxxxxxxxxxxxxxxxxxxxxx"  # replace the xxx with your api key here

''' # only run this once then afterwards use the pickle file so we don't have to query quandl API on every script run


usStates = pd.read_html('https://simple.wikipedia.org/wiki/List_of_U.S._states#List')

usStates = usStates[0]['postal abbreviation[1]']
```

```python
supFrame = pd.DataFrame()


for x in usStates['postal abbreviation[1]'][:]:

    qry = 'FMAC/HPI_'+str(x)+'.1'

    newdFrame = quandl.get(qry, authtoken=api_key)

    newdFrame.rename(columns={'NSA Value': str(x)}, inplace=True)

    # newdFrame[str(x)] = ( (newdFrame[str(x)] - newdFrame[str(x)][0]) / newdFrame[str(x)][0] ) * 100  # get percent change relative to starting value, enable this line if this percent values are to be saved

    if supFrame.empty:

        supFrame = newdFrame

    else:

        supFrame = supFrame.join(newdFrame)


supFrame.to_pickle('supFrame.pickle')

#supFrame.to_pickle('supFrame2.pickle') enable this line if this percent values are to be saved
```

'''

iniPercSupFrame = pd.read_pickle('supFrame2.pickle') # this is the dataframe with percent change relative to starting value

'''relpercSupFrame = supFrame.pct_change() # this calculates the percent change relative to the previous value

supFrame = pd.read_pickle('supFrame.pickle')

print(supFrame.head())

print(supFrame.tail())

print(relpercSupFrame.head())

print(relpercSupFrame.tail())

print(iniPercSupFrame.head())

print(iniPercSupFrame.tail())'''

'''supFrame.plot()

#relpercSupFrame.plot()

#iniPercSupFrame.plot()

style.use('fivethirtyeight')

plt.legend().remove()

plt.show()'''

''' # only run this once then afterwards use the pickle file so we don't have to query quandl API on every script run

usFrame = quandl.get('FMAC/HPI_USA.1', authtoken=api_key)

usFrame['NSA Value'] = ((usFrame['NSA Value'] - usFrame['NSA Value'][0]) / usFrame['NSA Value'][0]) * 100 # get percent change relative to starting value

usFrame.to_pickle('usFrame.pickle')'''

usFrame = pd.read_pickle('usFrame.pickle') # this has housing price index for the entire of USA

fig = plt.figure(figsize=(12, 10))

ax1 = plt.subplot2grid((1, 1), (0, 0))

style.use('fivethirtyeight')

#iniPercSupFrame.plot(ax=ax1)

#usFrame.plot(ax=ax1, color='k', linewidth=10)

#plt.legend().remove()

#plt.show() # the graph shows that there is definitely correlation between HPI of different states and also of states and the national HPI

stateHPIcorr = iniPercSupFrame.corr()   # find correlation of each state with the other states

print(stateHPIcorr.head())

print(stateHPIcorr.describe())   # get a summary of the dataframe

#stateYR = iniPercSupFrame['TX'].resample('A').mean()

stateYR = iniPercSupFrame['TX'].resample('A').ohlc()   # get open, high, low and close along with the monthly HPI for the state of Texas

print(stateYR.head())

iniPercSupFrame['TX'].plot(ax=ax1, label='Monthly TX HPI')

stateYR.plot(ax=ax1, label='Yearly TX HPI')

plt.legend(loc=4) # to show legend at bottom right hand side of the plot plt.show() # show relation between monthly HPI and annual mean HPI for the state of Texas

Note that I have commented out some parts of the code, uncomment them when you run the script for the first time. The outputs are below.

```
         AL        AK        AZ  ...        WV        WI        WY
AL 1.000000  0.956590  0.946930  ...  0.986657  0.992753  0.957353

AK 0.956590  1.000000  0.926650  ...  0.977033  0.943584  0.989444

AZ 0.946930  0.926650  1.000000  ...  0.933585  0.945189  0.927794

AR 0.995986  0.974277  0.946899  ...  0.993022  0.988525  0.971418

CA 0.949688  0.935188  0.982345  ...  0.946577  0.951628  0.935299


[5 rows x 50 columns]
         AL        AK        AZ  ...        WV        WI        WY
```

count 50.000000 50.000000 50.000000 ... 50.000000 50.000000 50.000000

mean   0.971637   0.947688   0.943983   ... 0.967408   0.967758   0.948303

std   0.022655   0.034883   0.022095   ... 0.027050   0.022545   0.036489

min   0.895294   0.814556   0.884497   ... 0.862753   0.901193   0.813296

25%   0.958299   0.937193   0.934415   ... 0.956899   0.954704   0.935313

50%   0.976359   0.955945   0.945212   ... 0.973251   0.971728   0.958090

75%   0.987204   0.965108   0.953891   ... 0.985205   0.985719   0.968983

max   1.000000   1.000000   1.000000   ... 1.000000   1.000000   1.000000

[8 rows x 50 columns]

Date   open high low   close

```
1975-12-31  0.000000   5.727672   0.000000   5.637840

1976-12-31  5.956903  13.843932   5.956903  13.843932

1977-12-31 14.362016  28.585277  14.362016  28.585277

1978-12-31 29.814172  48.705961  29.814172  48.705961

1979-12-31 50.274852  74.032622  50.274852  74.032622
```

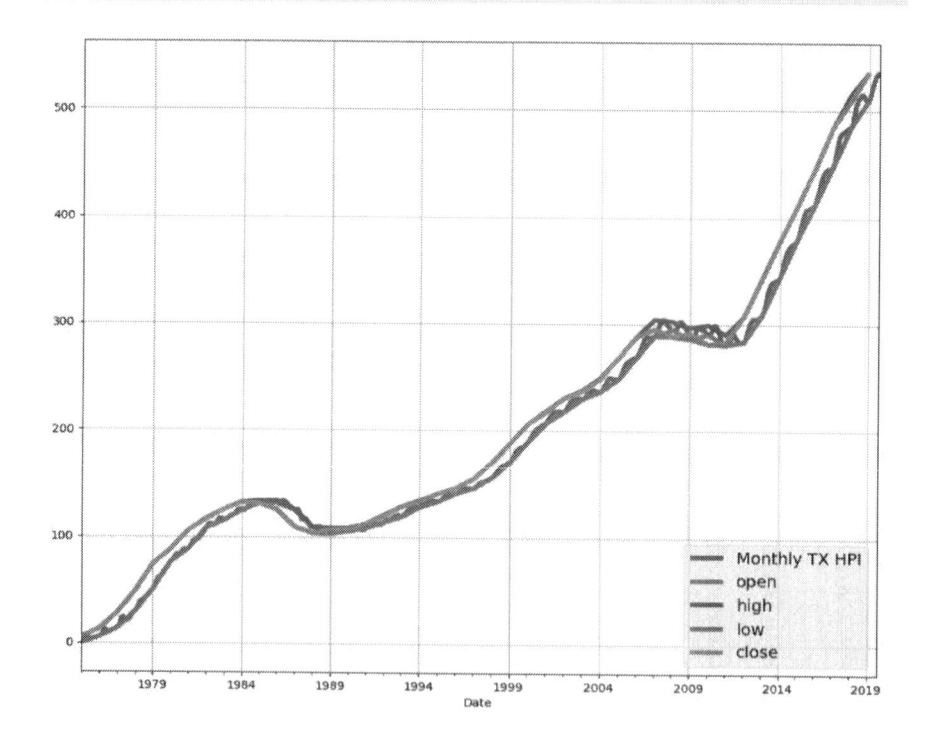

The next phase is to introduce some more data attributes and then perform machine learning to make some predictions.

''' # only run this once, then afterwards use the pickle file so we don't have to query quandl API on every script run

```
mortggFrame = quandl.get('FMAC/MORTG',
trim_start="1975-01-01", authtoken=api_key)

mortggFrame['Value'] = ((mortggFrame['Value'] -
mortggFrame['Value'][0]) / mortggFrame['Value'][0]) * 100  #
get percent change relative to starting value

print(mortggFrame.head())

mortggFrame = mortggFrame.resample('D').mean()

mortggFrame = mortggFrame.resample('M').mean()   # these
two resampling operations is a hack to shift data column from
start of month to end of month

print(mortggFrame.head())



mortggFrame.to_pickle('mortggFrame.pickle')'''



mortggFrame = pd.read_pickle('mortggFrame.pickle')

mortggFrame.columns = ['Mort30yr']

print(mortggFrame.head())
```

```
''' only run this once, then afterwards use the pickle file so we don't have to query quandl API on every script run

unEmp = quandl.get("USMISERY/INDEX.1", start_date="1975-01-31", authtoken=api_key)

unEmp["Unemployment Rate"] = ((unEmp["Unemployment Rate"] - unEmp["Unemployment Rate"][0]) / unEmp["Unemployment Rate"][0]) * 100.0  # get percent change relative to starting value


unEmp.to_pickle('unEmp.pickle')
'''

unEmp = pd.read_pickle('unEmp.pickle')

print(unEmp.head())



HPIMega = iniPercSupFrame.join([mortggFrame, unEmp])


HPIMega.dropna(inplace=True)  # remove all rows that have even one NaN

print(HPIMega)
```

HPIMega.to_pickle('HPIMega.pickle')

HPIMega = pd.read_pickle('HPIMega.pickle')

The "HPIMega.pickle" is our final prepared data that we will use to perform machine learning. The outputs generated by this section of code are:

Date   Mort30yr

1975-01-31 0.000000

1975-02-28 -3.393425

1975-03-31 -5.620361

1975-04-30 -6.468717

1975-05-31 -5.514316

Date   Unemployment Rate

1975-01-31   0.000000

1975-02-28   0.000000

1975-03-31   6.172840

1975-04-30   8.641975

1975-05-31   11.111111

Date	AL	AK	...	Mort30yr	Unemployment Rate
1975-01-31	0.000000	0.000000	...	0.000000	0.000000
1975-02-28	0.572095	1.461717	...	-3.393425	0.000000
1975-03-31	1.238196	2.963317	...	-5.620361	6.172840
1975-04-30	2.043555	4.534809	...	-6.468717	8.641975
1975-05-31	2.754944	6.258447	...	-5.514316	11.111111
...	...	... ...	...	...	
2016-05-31	266.360987	411.870585	...	-61.823966	-41.975309
2016-06-30	269.273949	412.844893	...	-62.142100	-39.506173
2016-07-31	271.680625	411.627829	...	-63.520679	-39.506173
2016-08-31	272.869925	409.194858	...	-63.520679	-39.506173

2016-09-30 272.330718 406.662586 ... -63.308590   -38.271605

[501 rows x 52 columns]

Let's start with some machine learning. You can backup all the code we've used up until now in another file or start with a new file from here on because we have gathered the prepared data in a pickle. The new file can import the pickle with these two lines of code.

import pandas as pd

HPIMega = pd.read_pickle('HPIMega.pickle')

We have to also install scikit-learn library to perform machine learning operations. Go to the Terminal section of PyCharm and run command "activate tf" if "tf" virtual environment is not active. Then, run the pip command.

pip install scikit-learn

Here is the code.

import pandas as pd

import numpy as np

```python
from statistics import mean

from sklearn import svm, preprocessing, model_selection


def addLabel(curHPI, futHPI):

    if futHPI > curHPI:

        return 1

    else:

        return 0


def movAvg(values):

    return mean(values)


HPIMega = pd.read_pickle('HPIMega.pickle')

HPIMega.rename(columns={"NSA    Value":    "US_HPI"}, inplace=True)

HPIMega = HPIMega.pct_change()  # because to predict future we should have percent change relative to last value not the start value
```

```python
HPIMega.replace([-np.inf, np.inf], np.nan, inplace=True)  # replace infinities with NaN

HPIMega['HPI_US_Fut'] = HPIMega['US_HPI'].shift(-1)


HPIMega.dropna(inplace=True)  # remove all NaN values

HPIMega['label'] = list(map(addLabel, HPIMega['US_HPI'], HPIMega['HPI_US_Fut']))


#HPIMega['custom_mort_mean'] = HPIMega['Mort30yr'].rolling(10).apply(movAvg, raw=True)  # example of rolling apply


# features are 'Mort30yr' and 'Unemployment Rate'


X = preprocessing.scale(np.array(HPIMega.drop(['label', 'HPI_US_Fut'], 1)))

y = np.array(HPIMega['label'])

X_train, X_Test, y_train, y_test = model_selection.train_test_split(X, y, test_size=0.2)  # 20% of
```

the data is reserved for testing instead of being used completely for training

```
cLinFunc = svm.SVC(kernel='linear')
```

```
cLinFunc.fit(X_train, y_train)
```

```
print("Predicting accuracy: %.2f%%" % (cLinFunc.score(X_Test, y_test)*100))
```

The above code gives the following output.

Prediction accuracy: 71.23%

The accuracy will fluctuate within a certain range. So a recap: we have written a script that predicts the labels 0 and 1. Remember that label would only be 1 if future HPI is greater than current HPI (meaning the real estate prices will go higher in the future). Our script correctly predicted on roughly 71 instances out of 100 tries when the HPI will rise or drop in the future. We can use some more data to the system, for example, US GDP, to further enhance the accuracy.

Are you going to meet the real estate tycoon with your current prediction model now or ask for more time, get more data, improve accuracy, and then have a meeting? What are you going to do?

Chapter 3: Working with Raspberry Pi

Ever heard of an overkill? Your computer or laptop might be a versatile beast, but sometimes it can feel like using a tank to go to Walmart. Depending upon your application, it might be easier to deal with a smaller, reprogrammable computer that offers a specific set of hardware capabilities. There have been various compact reprogrammable computers available for decades that engineers and coding enthusiasts have used to develop various solutions. Raspberry Pi is also one such computers.

What is Raspberry Pi?

Raspberry Pi is a credit-card-sized (a little thicker to be honest) minicomputer that can be programmed to perform any actions. Three features make Raspberry Pi standout from the competition:

1. Uses Python as coding language, which is much easier and powerful at the same time.
2. Smaller size, which makes it ideal for on-to-go applications that offer less power and space.
3. Readily accessible I/O ports to interact with other systems.

The applications of Raspberry Pi are so numerous that describing each one needs a separate book. The most common uses coders have found for this computer are

- automate home appliances
- remote control garage door
- control a robot to perform various tasks
- adding security system to your house
- add features to your car such as your own custom digital infotainment system

Selecting the Model

The current model of Raspberry Pi is 4 Model B. For this book, we are going to use the more common Model 3 B because you will find more content about this model on the internet. You can purchase the minicomputer by finding authorized resellers for your country on this web page
https://www.raspberrypi.org/products/raspberry-pi-3-model-b/

You will also have to purchase some peripherals. Here is a list.

1. A breadboard
2. A jumper wires kit (male to female is what we require for this book)
3. A bunch of LED lights (green, yellow, red)
4. A bunch of resistors (one 1k Ω, one 2k Ω, three 300-1k Ω)
5. Distance sensor (two HC-SR04)

6. Raspberry Pi camera module
7. A USB microSD card reader for your computer if it doesn't have a reader slot
8. A microUSB power supply (2.1 A rating)
9. A microSD card with at least 16GB of storage capacity and an adapter if you have purchased an older model
10. For development, you will need a monitor, keyboard, and mouse

Hardware Components

The Model 3 B replaced the Model 2 B in early 2016. It has the following hardware configuration:

- Quad Core 64bit CPU 1.2gHz Broadcom BCM2837
- 1GB Ram
- Wireless LAN and Bluetooth Low Energy (BLE) BCM43438 on board
- 100 Base Ethernet
- 40-pin GPIO (extended)
- 4 USB v2 ports
- Composite video port
- 4 Pole stereo audio port
- Full size HDMI
- CSI port to connect Raspberry Pi camera
- CSI port to connect Raspberry Pi touchscreen display
- MicroSD port

- MicroUSB power point that supports up to 2.5 A rated power sources

According to the manufacturers, this particular model complies with following European standards.

1. Electromagnetic Compatibility Directive (EMC) 2014/30/EU
2. Restriction of Hazardous Substances (RoHS) Directive 2011/65/EU

First Project

The codes in this section are inspired by the work of "sentdex" Youtube channel. The images used are also provided by the channel.

Installation and Setup

Go to the https://www.raspberrypi.org/downloads/ and select the NOOBS because that's the easier option to install the software. Installing Raspbian OS directly on the Raspberry Kit is a bit overwhelming and not advised for someone who is just starting with Raspberry Pi.. You will be redirected to https://www.raspberrypi.org/downloads/noobs/ and from there, select the NOOBS option. The NOOB Lite is faster to download but takes longer to install on the Raspberry kit.

When the download is finished, extract the files from the zipped folder. Before you flush the contents of the extracted folder to the microSD card for Raspberry Pi, you need to correctly format the microSD card. Download and install the official SD card formatter from https://www.sdcard.org/downloads/formatter/ for your operating system.

Plug in the SD card to your computer and start the formatter, select the correct Drive, click on the "Option" button and select "Full (Erase)" instead of "Quick" for the "Format Type". Also, select "On" for the "Format Size Adjustment". Click on "Ok" and then "Format". Click "Ok" if you are asked to confirm the action. It might take a minute for the formatting to complete, exit the formatter application.

Let's copy the contents of extracted NOOBS folder and paste it to the microSD drive. It can take some time as the files are in gigabytes. To turn on and off the Raspberry Pi, you simply plug in or out the power cord. For this reason, you should connect all peripherals before you plug in the power because if you connect the peripheral later, it might not get recognized. Once the copy/paste operation is complete, we have to plug the microSD card in the Raspberry Pi memory card slot which is on the bottom side of the kit. Let's connect a monitor and keyboard to the kit as well and plug in the power. A red LED light will turn on the Raspberry Pi, indicating it's turned on. You will see installation wizard start on the monitor.

Go through the installation wizard and let the operating system installation finish. It can take between 10-30 minutes for the process to complete. Once the installation is complete, you will see the Raspbian desktop on the monitor. Just like Windows, you can change the desktop background if you prefer but that's totally optional.

We have to update all the firmware of the Raspberry kit to the latest version. For that, you need to connect the kit with WiFi (you can also plugin an Ethernet cable if you don't have WiFi). On the top left corner of your screen, you will see an icon beside the Bluetooth icon that will show two lines with red crosses. Click on that icon; a small popup will appear listing all the available WiFi networks. Connect to your WiFi by entering the WiFi password if set. Once connected to WiFi, open the terminal by pressing CTRL + ALT + T and run the following command.

sudo apt-get update

Then,

sudo apt-get upgrade

Hopefully, the process will finish without any issues. But, if the update fails, you have to perform a few prerequisite tasks (correct the update distribution source link). Open the sources.list using the following command on the terminal:

sudo nano /etc/apt/sources.list

Once the file is open, replace everything with the following two commands. (Hint: Use CTRL+k to delete a line).

deb http://archive.raspbian.org/raspbian jessie main contrib non-free

deb-src http://archive.raspbian.org/raspbian jessie main contrib non-free

Use CTRL+X to close the file and select "Yes" when the system asks you to save the file.

Press "Enter" again to keep the same filename. Let's try upgrading the distribution.

sudo apt-get dist-upgrade

After it's completed successfully, we should rerun the original update and upgrade commands. But, first, we should purge wolfram engine from the system because it takes a lot of storage and doesn't have any benefits.

sudo apt-get purge wolfram

Enter 'y' to confirm and it will be deleted from the memory card. One more command to run here is, again enter 'y' to confirm.

sudo apt-get autoremove

Once that's finished execution, let's get back to updating and upgrading.

sudo apt-get update

sudo apt-get upgrade

Tip: if you want to break a process, press CTRL+C.

Remote Access to Raspberry Pi

We can access Raspberry Pi remotely on the same (local) network through two major methods.

1. Remote desktop
2. Secure Shell (SSH)

In both methods, the first step is to make sure the Raspberry Pi is connected to your wifi network.

SSH Method

We start by opening the terminal by pressing CTRL+ALT+T and running the following commands.

ifconfig

You will see details about your internet connection. You are looking for the "inet addr" which is your local IP address. Grab that IP address and then we have to enable the SSH because it's disabled by default. Open the Raspberry configuration with the following command.

sudo raspi-config

Navigate to "Interfacing Options", select "SSH", you will be asked to confirm, select "Yes" and SSH will be enabled. Select "Finish" to close the Raspberry configuration. We can now remotely connect our computer with Raspberry Pi. On Windows, we will require to download an application called Putty. Here is the URL https://www.chiark.greenend.org.uk/~sgtatham/putty/latest.html select the correct version that matches your Windows system. Once downloaded, install and start Putty. Note that the latest Windows 10 version supports SSH by default so you might want to update your Windows if you don't want to install Putty.

On the Putty screen, enter the IP address you collected from the Raspberry Pi and hit "Enter". You will see a new black window. Use "pi" in the "login as" and enter "raspberry" when asked for the password (these are the default values so every time you connect using this information you will be shown warning to change the login credentials). The connection will be established, you might be asked to confirm a few things, select "Yes" to finish setting up the remote connection.

Remote Desktop

This method is relatively easier to setup on Windows. If you are using the latest Windows version, this option is also included by default. You just need to install a remote desktop client on the Raspberry Pi. We are going to use "xrdp". Let's install using the following command.

sudo apt-get install tightvncserver

And then,

sudo apt-get install xrdp

If you try to install "xrdp" client and it doesn't go through, you might want to remove a few (Virtual Network Computing) VNC servers that are already added to the Raspberry Pi. Use the following command to do so.

sudo apt-get remove xrdp vnc4server tightvncserver

Once the installation is complete, let's start "Remote Desktop" application on Windows and enter the local IP address we had gathered before. Click "Yes" if you are asked to confirm anything. After a few moments, you will see a login screen, use "pi" and "raspberry" in the username and password fields, respectively. You will see a screen showing a lot of updates, and if everything goes right, you will see the Raspberry Pi desktop on your computer screen. Congratulations, the connection is set.

Two important commands before we start doing some fun stuff. To reboot the Raspberry Pi, use the following command.

sudo reboot

To completely shutdown the kit, use the following command.

sudo shutdown -h now

Using Camera with Raspberry Pi

Raspberry camera was last updated in spring 2016. It is an 8MP (Mega Pixel) Sony IMX219 sensor camera that supports capture of high definition video and images. You can also perform advanced video effects like time-lapse and slow-motion. The new camera has better image quality even in low-lit environments and exceptional color fidelity. The supported video formats are 1080p on 60 frames/sec, 720p on 60 frames/sec and the low-quality VGA90 that's suitable for long video recording that can clog the memory.

Let's plug the camera in the special camera slot and connect all other peripherals before powering up the Raspberry Pi. Once everything's ready, login to the Raspberry OS using the remote connection. Open the terminal and run the following command.

cd Desktop/

We also have to enable camera interfacing by starting Raspberry Configuration.

sudo raspi-config

Select "Interfacing Options", "Camera" is the first option, select it, select "Yes" to enable camera interface. Select "Finish" to close the configuration. You might have to reboot the Raspberry Pi, go ahead if it needs to be done. Once it powers back on, run the following command again if needed.

cd Desktop/

Run another command to create a script file on the desktop.

nano cameraex.py

This will open the script file. Let's add the following script.

import picamera

import time

cam = picamera.PiCamera()

cam.capture('firstImage.jpg')

Enter CTRL+X to close the script file, save it with the same name, and run the script using the terminal with the following command.

python cameraex.py

On the desktop, there will be a new image file. Open it to see the result. We can perform various image manipulations. For example, to vertically flip the image, we can change the "cameraex.py" script like this.

import picamera

import time

cam = picamera.PiCamera()

cam.vflip = True

cam.capture('firstImage.jpg')

Let's record a video. We have to replace the cam.capture() with another line of code.

import picamera

import time

cam = picamera.PiCamera()

#cam.vflip = True

#cam.capture('firstImage.jpg')

cam.start_recording('firstvid.h264')

time.sleep(5)

cam.stop_recording

Let's run the script using the following command.

python cameraex.py

To view the video, we need to use a media player. Raspbarian OS comes loaded with media player called "OMX Player". Let's call it in the terminal to view the recorded video.

```
omxplayer firstvid.h264
```

We can also test the camera with a live feed. Remove all the code from the script file and add the following lines, run the script from the terminal.

```
import picamera


cam = picamera.PiCamera()

cam.start_preview()
```

You should see a live video feed on your screen now. It might take a few seconds to appear. Also, if you are remotely running the Raspberry OS, make sure the monitor connected with the Raspberry Pi is turned on because all the images and videos only show up in that monitor, not on the remotely connected system monitor.

Sending and Receiving Signals Using GPIO of the Raspberry Pi

Sending Signal

Let's set up a series circuit on the breadboard using a 300-1k Ω resistor, a red LED (you can choose any other color), and the two male to female jumpers. If you have no idea how to create circuits on a breadboard, here's a tutorial that can get you up to speed https://www.youtube.com/watch?v=6WReFkfrUIk.

Make sure you remember the pins where you connect the female end of jumpers on the GPIO. To make things easier, let's connect the female end of jumper at the GPIO23 position. Here is the map of GPIO pins on the Raspberry Pi to make more sense.

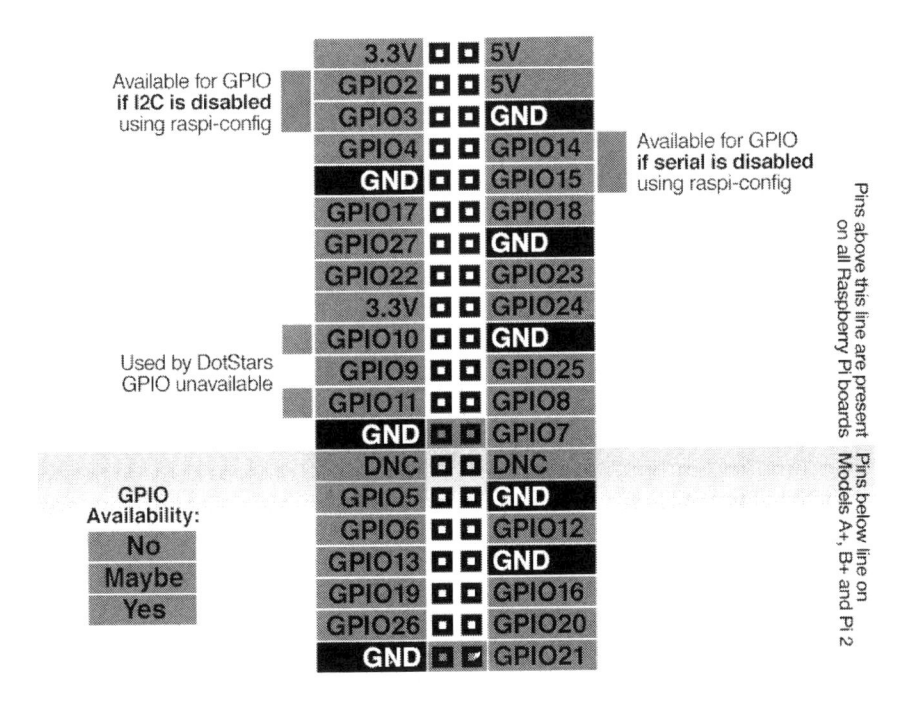

Once the circuit is ready, power up the Raspberry Pi and let's start with the coding. Open the terminal, navigate to the desktop and just to double check, we will install the GPIO RPI using the following command.

sudo apt-get install python-rpi.gpio

If the RPI is already installed, the terminal will let you know. Let's create a script file "ledex.py" and add the following script to it.

import RPI.GPIO as GPIO

import time

female end of jumper connected at GPIO23

GPIO.setmode(GPIO.BCM)

GPIO.setup(23, GPIO.OUT)

GPIO.output(23, GPIO.HIGH)

time.sleep(5)

GPIO.output(23, GPIO.LOW)

GPIO.cleanup()

Save the script file and run it through the terminal using the following command.

python ledex.py

You will be able to see the LED light up for 5 seconds and then turn off.

Receiving Signal

Let's create a circuit using the HC SR04 distance sensor, four jumpers, and three 1k Ω resistors. How does the distance sensor work? We can send a sound signal (trigger) using the sensor which strikes a physical object in front of the sensor and is received back by the sensor (echo). Since we know the speed of sound, we can calculate the time difference between the trigger and echo to calculate the distance between the sensor and the physical object.

Once everything is connected as shown in the image below, power up the kit and start the terminal to run a few commands.

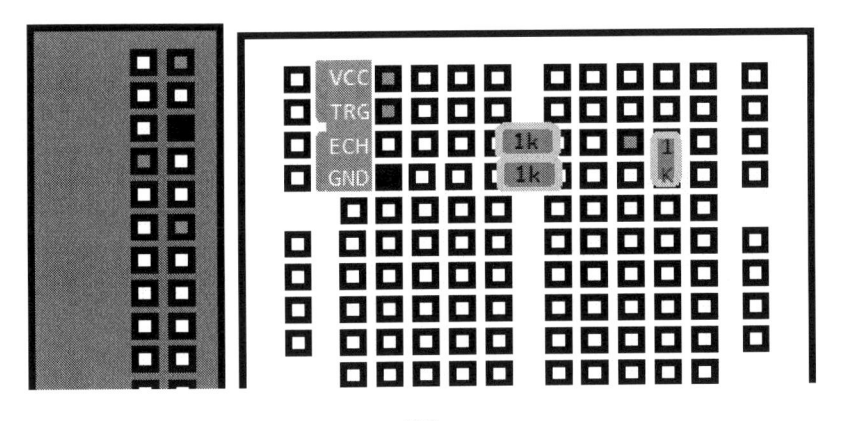

cd Desktop/

nano distancesensor.py

In the new script file, add the following script.

import RPI.GPIO as GPIO

import time

GPIO.setmode(GPIO.BCM)

TRIG = 4 # GPIO pin number where trigger of distance sensor is connected

ECHO = 18 # GPIO pin number where echo of distance sensor is connected

GPIO.setup(TRIG, GPIO.OUT)

GPIO.setup(ECHO, GPIO.IN)

GPIO.output(TRIG, True)

time.sleep(0.0005)

```
GPIO.output(TRIG, False)

while GPIO.input(ECHO) == False:

    strtP = time.time()

while GPIO.input(ECHO) == True:

    endP = time.time()

travlTime = endP - strtP

distance = travlTime / 0.000058

print('Distance: %.2f cm', % (distance))

GPIO.cleanup()
```

Back on the terminal, run the script with the following command.

```
python distancesensor.py
```

Now, let's move on to the real purpose of this project, to create an automatic garage stop light that will be activated when you pull your car into the garage. The light should be green if there's space in the garage, turn yellow as the car moves closer and turn red when there's no space.

The circuit should be setup according to the given figure.

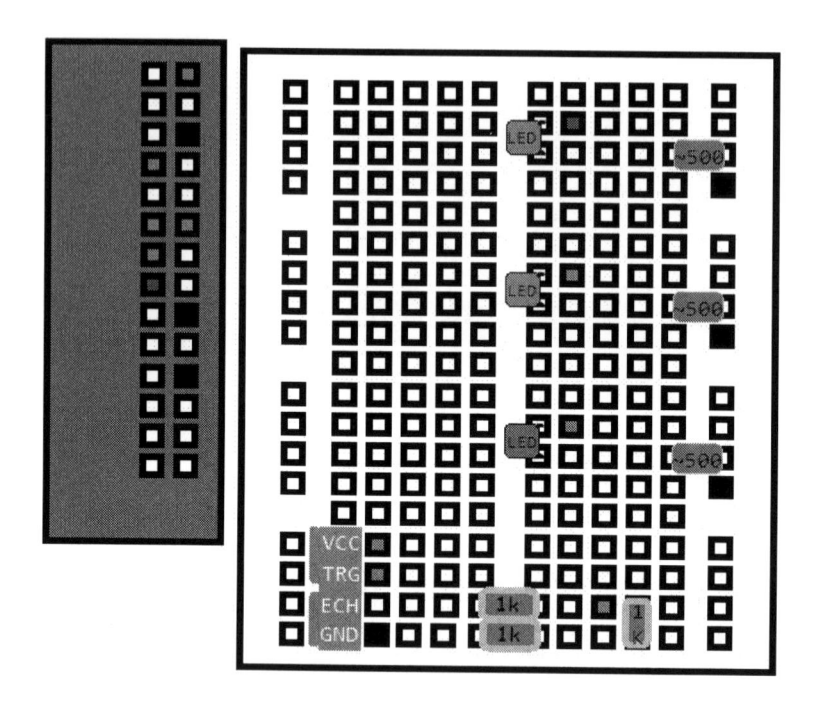

After making the connections, power up the Raspberry Pi and create a new script file to host the following script.

import RPi.GPIO as GPIO

import time

GPIO.setwarnings(False) # doing this first, since we're using a while True.

GPIO.cleanup() # this resets the pins in the GPIO port

```
GPIO.setmode(GPIO.BCM)

# declaring pin connections

TRIG = 4

ECHO = 18

GREEN = 17

YELLOW = 27

RED = 22


# declaring input and output signals

GPIO.setup(TRIG,GPIO.OUT)

GPIO.setup(ECHO,GPIO.IN)


GPIO.setup(GREEN,GPIO.OUT)

GPIO.setup(YELLOW,GPIO.OUT)

GPIO.setup(RED,GPIO.OUT)


def greenLEDon():
```

```
    GPIO.output(GREEN, GPIO.HIGH)

    GPIO.output(YELLOW, GPIO.LOW)

    GPIO.output(RED, GPIO.LOW)


def yellowLEDon():

    GPIO.output(GREEN, GPIO.LOW)

    GPIO.output(YELLOW, GPIO.HIGH)

    GPIO.output(RED, GPIO.LOW)


def redLEDon():

    GPIO.output(GREEN, GPIO.LOW)

    GPIO.output(YELLOW, GPIO.LOW)

    GPIO.output(RED, GPIO.HIGH)


def getDistance():   # this is the code we developed before

    GPIO.output(TRIG, True)

    time.sleep(0.000005)
```

```python
GPIO.output(TRIG, False)

while GPIO.input(ECHO) == False:
    strtP = time.time()

while GPIO.input(ECHO) == True:
    endP = time.time()

travlTime = endP - startP

# getting distance in centimeters
distance = travlTime / 0.000058

#print('Distance: %.2f cms' %(distance))

return distance
```

```
while True:

    distance = getDistance()

    time.sleep(0.005)

    print(distance)


    if distance >= 30:

    greenLEDon()

    elif 30 > distance > 10:

    yellowLEDon()

    elif distance <= 10:

    redLEDon()
```

You can test this script by moving your hand closer and further from the sensor. We can build upon this to create a script that will automatically open and close the garage door when you pull up on the driveway. Can you think of how machine learning can make these scripts give better results? Maybe the distance measured over a period of time can be analyzed to profile your driving behavior and make accurate predictions like how fast you would be pulling up in the garage on a Monday evening coming back from work!

The above simple project was just an example showcasing the power of Raspberry Pi. Feel free to experiment with Raspberry Pi and take on some projects. Here are a few cool examples.

1. Create a weather station that monitors atmospheric parameters and makes predictions.
2. Create a social media bot. You can work with Twitter as it's a bit easier.
3. Create a Minecraft game server. Good thing is, this project doesn't require much hardware investment.
4. Create a time-lapse camera. Everyone loves taking cool videos!

Chapter 4: Working with TensorFlow

Remember we briefly talked about TensorFlow at the start of this book but left it for later? Well, it's time to learn everything about TensorFlow. So, what is TensorFlow? TensorFlow is a Python library for machine learning and scientific computing. We have already set up all the requirements, so let's get started with a hands-on project.

The Projects

As a demonstration of how TensorFlow can be used to implement machine learning in a real-life scenario, we will focus on a large data set that contains student attributes along with previous grades and successfully train and test a model to make accurate predictions on student performance in high school.

On PyCharm, go ahead and close all open projects. Now, you will see the initial window and on the left sidebar, you will see the "tensorEnv" project, click on it to open. This is the project we will be working on for this chapter.

To download the data, go to the link https://archive.ics.uci.edu/ml/datasets/Student+Performance and click on highlighted "Data Folder". In the new page, select "student.zip" and download to the folder anywhere on your computer. Now, unzip the folder and grab the student-met.csv file and move it to the working directory of the "tensorEnv" current project.

Project #1: Predicting Student Grade

We have to prepare the data set before creating a model based on it. We will look to eliminate rows and/or columns that have missing data and discard student attributes that we consider surplus. An important note: do not discard too much data or you might end up with very bad prediction scores. The more data you have, the more chances of creating an accurate prediction model.

For our project, we are going to relate the past student grades with their weekly study time (studytime), previous class failures (failures), and school absences (absences) to predict their future grade.

import pandas as pd

import numpy as np

import sklearn

from sklearn import linear_model

stdntFram = pd.read_csv('student-mat.csv', delimiter=";") # usually files have ',' as delimiter so we don't need to set this but in this file, we have to declare the correct data delimiter

```python
#print(stdntFram.head())  # check the data frame to see if we need to prepare the data before building the model


# G1, G2, G3 are the semester grades for every student


stdntFram = stdntFram[['G1', 'G2', 'G3', 'studytime', 'failures', 'absences']]  # discarding data that's currently irrelevant to our current project requirements. You might want to experiment by keeping a few more attributes and see if prediction scores get better


predict = 'G3'  # goal is to predict this as close to the actual values, will remove this column from stdntFram before training and testing


X = np.array(stdntFram.drop([predict], 1))

y = np.array(stdntFram[predict])


X_train, X_test, y_train, y_test = sklearn.model_selection.train_test_split(X, y, test_size=0.2)  #
```

segment data set between training and testing data, 20% testing data is the standard

linMod = linear_model.LinearRegression()   # choose a model, linear in this case

linMod.fit(X_train, y_train) # train the model

accuracy = linMod.score(X_test, y_test)

print("Prediction accuracy: %.2f%%" % (accuracy * 100))   # will fluctuate within a range on subsequent script executions

allPred = linMod.predict(X_test)

for itr in range(len(allPred)):

    print(allPred[itr], X_test[itr], y_test[itr])   # first is predicted by our system and last value is what the value actually is

Look at the data closely and see what other observations you can make. Modify the script to use more attributes and see if how closely other attributes relate to the grades and if prediction accuracy can be further improved.

Prediction accuracy: 87.09%

6.754745900887105 [7 8 4 0 8] 8

13.109798237848533 [14 13 3 1 12] 13

3.632451977653248 [6 5 3 1 0] 0

4.3744867252888895 [6 5 1 0 7] 6

Project #2: Predicting Student Grade

Let's take on another project. This time we are going to implement the K-Nearest Neighbors (KNN) algorithm to relate an integer 'k' with its closest neighbors. We are going to deal with a data set that will require more preprocessing than we did in the earlier project. The KNN algorithm is usually used to classify data points, for example, a movies database can be modeled to learn about good and bad movies and predict a future movie's classification as bad or good. In our project, we are going to classify cars in view of certain car attributes.

Let's go to https://archive.ics.uci.edu/ml/data sets/Car+Evaluation and download the "Car Evaluation Data Set" as we did for the first project. We are going to add a header to this file that will make it easier to use pandas to read the data. Just open the data file in PyCharm and add the following line as the first line of the file. Don't forget to save the file afterwards.

buying,maint,door,persons,lug_boot,safety,class

Let's start coding.

import sklearn

from sklearn.neighbors import KNeighborsClassifier

import pandas as pd

from sklearn import preprocessing

data = pd.read_csv("car.data")

#print(data.head()) # check the data frame to see if we need to prepare the data before building the model

lblEnc = preprocessing.LabelEncoder()

buying = lblEnc.fit_transform(list(data["buying"]))

maint = lblEnc.fit_transform(list(data["maint"]))

door = lblEnc.fit_transform(list(data["door"]))

```python
persons = lblEnc.fit_transform(list(data["persons"]))

lug_boot = lblEnc.fit_transform(list(data["lug_boot"]))

safety = lblEnc.fit_transform(list(data["safety"]))

clasify = lblEnc.fit_transform(list(data["class"]))


predict = "class"  # optional


X = list(zip(buying, maint, door, persons, lug_boot, safety))

y = list(clasify)


X_train, X_test, y_train, y_test = sklearn.model_selection.train_test_split(X, y, test_size=0.2)


knnModel = KNeighborsClassifier(n_neighbors=9)


knnModel.fit(X_train, y_train)
```

accuracy = knnModel.score(X_test, y_test)

print("Prediction accuracy: %.2f%%" % (accuracy * 100))

allPred = knnModel.predict(X_test)

classifyNames = ['unacc', 'acc', 'good', 'vgood']

for x in range(len(X_test)):
    print("Predicted value: ", classifyNames[allPred[x]], "Test data: ", X_test[x], "Actual data: ", classifyNames[y_test[x]])

The above code will output the following results.

Prediction accuracy: 90.46%

Predicted value: good Test data: (1, 3, 3, 1, 2, 1) Actual data: good

Predicted value: good Test data: (1, 0, 0, 0, 2, 0) Actual data: good

Predicted value: good Test data: (2, 1, 1, 0, 0, 1) Actual data: good

Predicted value: good Test data: (0, 3, 2, 2, 0, 0) Actual data: good

Predicted value: unacc Test data: (1, 1, 3, 1, 2, 2) Actual data: unacc

Predicted value: unacc Test data: (3, 1, 2, 2, 1, 2) Actual data: unacc

Predicted value: good Test data: (2, 0, 3, 1, 2, 1) Actual data: good

Predicted value: acc Test data: (1, 1, 3, 2, 0, 2) Actual data: acc

Predicted value: good Test data: (3, 0, 0, 1, 2, 1) Actual data: good

Predicted value: good Test data: (2, 0, 0, 0, 2, 2) Actual data: good

Predicted value: good Test data: (1, 1, 1, 2, 0, 1) Actual data: good

Predicted value: good Test data: (3, 0, 0, 1, 2, 0) Actual data: good

Predicted value: unacc Test data: (1, 1, 2, 2, 2, 2) Actual data: unacc

Predicted value: good Test data: (1, 2, 0, 1, 1, 1) Actual data: good

Predicted value: unacc Test data: (1, 0, 2, 1, 0, 2) Actual data: unacc

Predicted value: good Test data: (3, 2, 0, 0, 2, 0) Actual data: good

Predicted value: good Test data: (1, 2, 1, 1, 2, 1) Actual data: good

Predicted value: good Test data: (3, 3, 3, 2, 0, 1) Actual data: good

Predicted value: unacc Test data: (3, 1, 3, 1, 2, 0) Actual data: unacc

Predicted value: good Test data: (0, 3, 3, 0, 2, 2) Actual data: good

Predicted value: good Test data: (1, 3, 2, 1, 1, 2) Actual data: unacc

Predicted value: unacc Test data: (2, 3, 3, 2, 0, 0) Actual data: unacc

Predicted value: good Test data: (2, 0, 1, 0, 2, 2) Actual data: good

Predicted value: good Test data: (2, 1, 1, 0, 2, 2) Actual data: good

Predicted value: good Test data: (0, 2, 3, 1, 0, 0) Actual data: unacc

Predicted value: good Test data: (0, 2, 0, 1, 2, 2) Actual data: good

Predicted value: good Test data: (2, 0, 0, 0, 1, 1) Actual data: good

Predicted value: acc Test data: (1, 1, 2, 1, 0, 2) Actual data: acc

Predicted value: good Test data: (2, 3, 0, 2, 0, 0) Actual data: unacc

Predicted value: good Test data: (0, 3, 0, 0, 0, 1) Actual data: good

Predicted value: good Test data: (0, 0, 0, 0, 1, 0) Actual data: good

Predicted value: unacc Test data: (1, 2, 0, 1, 1, 0) Actual data: acc

Predicted value: good Test data: (1, 1, 0, 0, 1, 1) Actual data: good

Predicted value: good Test data: (0, 1, 0, 2, 2, 1) Actual data: good

Predicted value: good Test data: (0, 3, 1, 0, 1, 2) Actual data: good

Predicted value: good Test data: (3, 3, 2, 0, 2, 2) Actual data: good

Predicted value: good Test data: (2, 1, 0, 2, 2, 0) Actual data: good

Predicted value: unacc Test data: (2, 2, 1, 2, 0, 2) Actual data: unacc

Predicted value: good Test data: (0, 0, 1, 2, 0, 1) Actual data: good

Predicted value: good Test data: (2, 3, 1, 0, 1, 0) Actual data: good

Predicted value: good Test data: (3, 1, 1, 1, 2, 2) Actual data: good

Predicted value: good Test data: (2, 3, 0, 1, 0, 0) Actual data: unacc

Predicted value: acc Test data: (2, 1, 1, 1, 2, 0) Actual data: acc

Predicted value: good Test data: (3, 0, 3, 1, 0, 0) Actual data: good

Predicted value: good Test data: (2, 0, 1, 0, 2, 0) Actual data: good

Predicted value: good Test data: (1, 0, 2, 0, 1, 2) Actual data: good

Predicted value: good Test data: (0, 3, 0, 0, 2, 0) Actual data: good

Predicted value: good Test data: (3, 2, 0, 0, 1, 2) Actual data: good

Predicted value: good Test data: (0, 1, 0, 2, 0, 2) Actual data: unacc

Predicted value: good Test data: (0, 3, 3, 0, 1, 0) Actual data: good

Predicted value: good Test data: (3, 3, 0, 0, 1, 0) Actual data: good

Predicted value: good Test data: (3, 0, 2, 0, 2, 0) Actual data: good

Predicted value: good Test data: (0, 3, 3, 2, 2, 0) Actual data: good

Predicted value: good Test data: (1, 2, 0, 2, 1, 0) Actual data: acc

Predicted value: good Test data: (1, 1, 2, 1, 1, 1) Actual data: good

Predicted value: good Test data: (2, 2, 1, 1, 1, 2) Actual data: unacc

Predicted value: unacc Test data: (0, 1, 1, 1, 0, 0) Actual data: unacc

Predicted value: good Test data: (3, 1, 0, 1, 0, 0) Actual data: unacc

Predicted value: good Test data: (2, 0, 0, 2, 2, 1) Actual data: good

Predicted value: good Test data: (1, 2, 3, 0, 1, 1) Actual data: good

Predicted value: good Test data: (3, 2, 2, 0, 0, 1) Actual data: good

Predicted value: good Test data: (1, 2, 2, 0, 0, 1) Actual data: good

Predicted value: good Test data: (0, 2, 2, 1, 0, 0) Actual data: unacc

Predicted value: good Test data: (1, 0, 3, 0, 1, 0) Actual data: good

Predicted value: unacc Test data: (3, 2, 1, 1, 2, 0) Actual data: unacc

Predicted value: good Test data: (0, 0, 0, 0, 1, 2) Actual data: good

Predicted value: good Test data: (1, 3, 0, 2, 0, 0) Actual data: unacc

Predicted value: good Test data: (2, 3, 2, 1, 0, 1) Actual data: good

Predicted value: good Test data: (2, 2, 0, 1, 1, 1) Actual data: good

Predicted value: vgood Test data: (2, 1, 1, 2, 0, 0) Actual data: vgood

Predicted value: good Test data: (1, 3, 2, 2, 2, 1) Actual data: good

Predicted value: unacc Test data: (1, 1, 1, 1, 1, 2) Actual data: unacc

Predicted value: good Test data: (2, 3, 3, 0, 1, 1) Actual data: good

Predicted value: good Test data: (2, 3, 2, 0, 1, 2) Actual data: good

Predicted value: good Test data: (3, 0, 2, 2, 0, 1) Actual data: good

Predicted value: good Test data: (2, 2, 2, 2, 2, 1) Actual data: good

Predicted value: unacc Test data: (2, 1, 2, 2, 0, 2) Actual data: acc

Predicted value: good Test data: (3, 3, 1, 1, 2, 0) Actual data: good

Predicted value: unacc Test data: (2, 2, 3, 1, 0, 2) Actual data: unacc

Predicted value: good Test data: (3, 1, 0, 1, 0, 1) Actual data: good

Predicted value: good Test data: (3, 0, 1, 0, 1, 0) Actual data: good

Predicted value: good Test data: (2, 1, 0, 2, 0, 1) Actual data: good

Predicted value: unacc Test data: (2, 3, 2, 1, 2, 0) Actual data: unacc

Predicted value: good Test data: (0, 2, 0, 2, 2, 2) Actual data: good

Predicted value: unacc Test data: (2, 3, 3, 1, 0, 2) Actual data: unacc

Predicted value: good Test data: (2, 1, 2, 2, 2, 1) Actual data: good

Predicted value: good Test data: (3, 0, 3, 2, 2, 2) Actual data: good

Predicted value: acc Test data: (2, 1, 1, 2, 1, 0) Actual data: vgood

Predicted value: good Test data: (0, 3, 0, 1, 2, 0) Actual data: good

Predicted value: good Test data: (1, 1, 2, 0, 0, 0) Actual data: good

Predicted value: vgood Test data: (2, 1, 2, 2, 0, 0) Actual data: vgood

Predicted value: good Test data: (0, 3, 1, 0, 1, 1) Actual data: good

Predicted value: good Test data: (2, 1, 1, 0, 2, 0) Actual data: good

Predicted value: good Test data: (1, 3, 3, 0, 0, 1) Actual data: good

Predicted value: good Test data: (3, 0, 0, 2, 2, 1) Actual data: good

Predicted value: unacc Test data: (1, 0, 2, 2, 2, 0) Actual data: unacc

Predicted value: unacc Test data: (0, 0, 0, 2, 0, 0) Actual data: unacc

Predicted value: good Test data: (1, 1, 2, 0, 1, 2) Actual data: good

Predicted value: good Test data: (3, 3, 0, 2, 2, 0) Actual data: good

Predicted value: acc Test data: (2, 1, 2, 2, 1, 2) Actual data: acc

Predicted value: good Test data: (3, 3, 3, 0, 2, 1) Actual data: good

Predicted value: good Test data: (1, 3, 1, 0, 1, 0) Actual data: good

Predicted value: good Test data: (3, 3, 0, 1, 1, 0) Actual data: good

Predicted value: unacc Test data: (3, 1, 0, 1, 1, 0) Actual data: unacc

Predicted value: good Test data: (3, 1, 1, 0, 2, 0) Actual data: good

Predicted value: good Test data: (1, 1, 2, 2, 0, 1) Actual data: good

Predicted value: unacc Test data: (2, 2, 1, 1, 0, 2) Actual data: unacc

Predicted value: good Test data: (3, 3, 1, 0, 2, 0) Actual data: good

Predicted value: good Test data: (1, 0, 1, 2, 2, 1) Actual data: good

Predicted value: unacc Test data: (1, 1, 0, 1, 1, 2) Actual data: unacc

Predicted value: unacc Test data: (2, 0, 2, 1, 1, 0) Actual data: unacc

Predicted value: acc Test data: (1, 1, 2, 1, 2, 0) Actual data: acc

Predicted value: good Test data: (2, 3, 1, 0, 2, 2) Actual data: good

Predicted value: good Test data: (2, 1, 0, 0, 2, 2) Actual data: good

Predicted value: good Test data: (1, 3, 2, 1, 0, 1) Actual data: good

Predicted value: good Test data: (2, 0, 2, 1, 1, 1) Actual data: good

Predicted value: good Test data: (0, 0, 0, 0, 2, 0) Actual data: good

Predicted value: good Test data: (1, 0, 0, 0, 2, 1) Actual data: good

Predicted value: good Test data: (3, 1, 2, 0, 1, 1) Actual data: good

Predicted value: unacc Test data: (2, 1, 2, 2, 2, 2) Actual data: unacc

Predicted value: good Test data: (3, 2, 2, 1, 2, 1) Actual data: good

Predicted value: good Test data: (0, 2, 0, 1, 0, 1) Actual data: good

Predicted value: unacc Test data: (1, 2, 0, 1, 2, 0) Actual data: acc

Predicted value: good Test data: (3, 2, 0, 1, 1, 1) Actual data: good

Predicted value: good Test data: (0, 1, 0, 0, 2, 1) Actual data: good

Predicted value: good Test data: (1, 0, 2, 0, 1, 1) Actual data: good

Predicted value: good Test data: (2, 0, 3, 0, 0, 1) Actual data: good

Predicted value: good Test data: (0, 3, 1, 2, 1, 0) Actual data: good

Predicted value: good Test data: (1, 3, 2, 2, 2, 2) Actual data: good

Predicted value: good Test data: (1, 1, 0, 2, 1, 0) Actual data: acc

Predicted value: good Test data: (1, 2, 2, 2, 0, 1) Actual data: good

Predicted value: good Test data: (3, 1, 3, 0, 0, 1) Actual data: good

Predicted value: unacc Test data: (0, 2, 1, 2, 2, 0) Actual data: unacc

Predicted value: unacc Test data: (2, 3, 2, 2, 0, 2) Actual data: unacc

Predicted value: good Test data: (2, 3, 2, 0, 1, 1) Actual data: good

Predicted value: good Test data: (3, 3, 3, 1, 1, 1) Actual data: good

Predicted value: good Test data: (1, 2, 1, 2, 0, 1) Actual data: good

Predicted value: good Test data: (1, 0, 0, 0, 2, 2) Actual data: good

Predicted value: good Test data: (1, 2, 2, 0, 2, 1) Actual data: good

Predicted value: good Test data: (1, 3, 3, 0, 1, 1) Actual data: good

Predicted value: vgood Test data: (2, 0, 3, 2, 0, 0) Actual data: unacc

Predicted value: good Test data: (3, 0, 2, 0, 2, 1) Actual data: good

Predicted value: acc Test data: (2, 1, 0, 2, 0, 2) Actual data: acc

Predicted value: good Test data: (1, 1, 0, 1, 1, 0) Actual data: acc

Predicted value: good Test data: (0, 0, 1, 2, 2, 2) Actual data: good

Predicted value: good Test data: (0, 3, 2, 2, 2, 0) Actual data: good

Predicted value: good Test data: (2, 0, 3, 2, 1, 1) Actual data: good

Project #3: Neural Network using TensorFlow

In this project, we are going to create a neural network that will work on the TensorFlow Keras Fashion MNIST image data set to classify clothing images. We already have setup all the prerequisites so let's start with the coding.

Here's the code. I have added comments wherever necessary.

import tensorflow as tf

from tensorflow import keras

import numpy as np

```python
import matplotlib.pyplot as plt

imgData = keras.data sets.fashion_mnist  # import the image data set

(img_train, lbl_train), (img_test, lbl_test) = imgData.load_data()  # segment data set into training and testing data

# declaring available cloth types
cloth_type = ['T-shirt/top', 'Trouser', 'Pullover', 'Dress', 'Coat', 'Sandal', 'Shirt', 'Sneaker', 'Bag', 'Ankle Boot']

# normalizing images using scalar division
img_train = img_train / 255.0
img_test = img_test / 255.0

'''define model
```

- flatten = prepare image which is 2d/3d array so it can be passed through individual 1d neurons

- dense = fully connect all neurons to create a layer

- relu = input layer, rectified linear unit, we can use other activation function

- softmax = output layer, pick all neuron values in a way they add up to one (which also makes it show probability)

'''

neuralModel = keras.Sequential([

    keras.layers.Flatten(input_shape=(28, 28)),

  keras.layers.Dense(128, activation="relu"),

    keras.layers.Dense(10, activation="softmax")

])

create the model using the above definition, typical values are used for optimizer, loss and metrics

neuralModel.compile(optimizer="adam", loss="sparse_categorical_crossentropy", metrics=["accuracy"])

```
neuralModel.fit(img_train, lbl_train, epochs=5)  # using higher epochs doesn't improve the accuracy a lot


testLoss, testAcc = neuralModel.evaluate(img_test, lbl_test)

print("Tested Accuracy: %.2f%%" % (testAcc*100))


# perform prediction

allPred = neuralModel.predict(img_test)


# we can use following code to confirm our script is making correct predictions

for itr in range(5):

    plt.grid(False)

    plt.imshow(img_test[itr], cmap=plt.cm.binary)  # shows a better version of the image

    plt.xlabel("Actual: " + cloth_type[lbl_test[itr]])

    plt.title("Prediction:            " + cloth_type[np.argmax(allPred[itr])])

    plt.show()
```

The output of the above script is:

Tested Accuracy: 88.0%

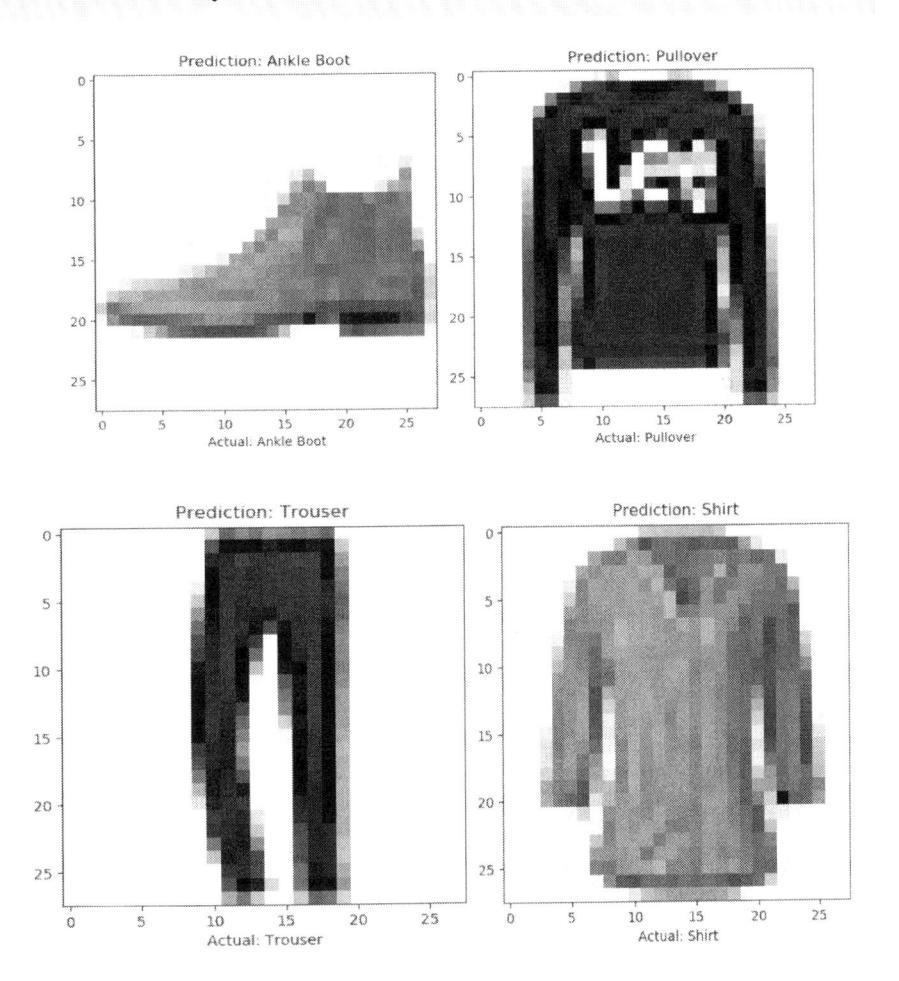

Chapter 5: Advanced Machine Learning

If you are starting the last chapter of this book, it means you have a high degree of understanding of all the underlying concepts of Python programming and machine learning. If that's not the case, it's highly recommended to revisit the previous chapters. This chapter is going to be short and direct. We are going to take on a corporate level project.

A Corporate Project

You have an online store and want to optimize the chat service your support staff uses, so outside office hours, a chat bot will take over chat service and offer answers to most common queries.

Create a Predictive Chat Bot

The chat bot will learn the user queries and over time provide better answers. Let's start coding without any delay. Go ahead and install the "nltk" and "tflearn" libraries in the virtual environment. I am going to use a json file to give training and testing data to our chat bot. I have filled the json file with some random strings that look like most common user queries during the chat in the past.

Here's the complete code inspired by the work of "techwithtim" Youtube channel. The chat bot will have to process natural language, in Python, we can use the nltk library for this purpose.

```python
import nltk

from nltk.stem.lancaster import LancasterStemmer

stemmer = LancasterStemmer()


import numpy

import tflearn

import tensorflow

import json

import pickle


with open("intents.json") as file:

    data = json.load(file)


try:

    with open("data.pickle", "rb") as f:
```

```python
        words, labels, training, output = pickle.load(f)
except:
    words = []
    labels = []
    docs_x = []
    docs_y = []

    for intent in data["intents"]:
        for pattern in intent["patterns"]:
            wrds = nltk.word_tokenize(pattern)
            words.extend(wrds)
            docs_x.append(wrds)
            docs_y.append(intent["tag"])

        if intent["tag"] not in labels:
            labels.append(intent["tag"])
```

```python
        words = [stemmer.stem(w.lower()) for w in words if w != "?"]

        words = sorted(list(set(words)))

        labels = sorted(labels)

        training = []

        output = []

        out_empty = [0 for _ in range(len(labels))]

        for x, doc in enumerate(docs_x):

            bag = []

            wrds = [stemmer.stem(w.lower()) for w in doc]

            for w in words:
```

```
if w in wrds:

    bag.append(1)

else:

    bag.append(0)


output_row = out_empty[:]

output_row[labels.index(docs_y[x])] = 1


training.append(bag)

output.append(output_row)


training = numpy.array(training)

output = numpy.array(output)


with open("data.pickle", "wb") as f:

    pickle.dump((words, labels, training, output), f)
```

```
tensorflow.reset_default_graph()


net = tflearn.input_data(shape=[None, len(training[0])])

net = tflearn.fully_connected(net, 8)

net = tflearn.fully_connected(net, 8)

net = tflearn.fully_connected(net, len(output[0]), activation="softmax")

net = tflearn.regression(net)


model = tflearn.DNN(net)


try:
    model.load("model.tflearn")
except:
    model.fit(training, output, n_epoch=1000, batch_size=8, show_metric=True)
    model.save("model.tflearn")
```

To start using the chat bot, we can add two functions to the script as shown below.

```python
def bag_of_words(s, words):

    bag = [0 for _ in range(len(words))]

    s_words = nltk.word_tokenize(s)

    s_words = [stemmer.stem(word.lower()) for word in s_words]

    for se in s_words:

        for i, w in enumerate(words):

            if w == se:

                bag[i] = 1

    return numpy.array(bag)

def chat():

    print("Start talking with the bot (type quit to stop)!")
```

```python
    while True:
        inp = input("You: ")
        if inp.lower() == "quit":
            break

        results = model.predict([bag_of_words(inp, words)])
        results_index = numpy.argmax(results)
        tag = labels[results_index]

        for tg in data["intents"]:
            if tg['tag'] == tag:
                responses = tg['responses']

        print(random.choice(responses))

chat()
```

Conclusion

I hope you enjoyed this book. We started from the basics of Python and worked towards implementing some pretty serious machine-learning concepts. I also hope that after reading this book, you feel content with my efforts and are motivated towards exploring more about machine learning on your own.

There are various resources available online that you can follow to further your journey in this field. You will find several good YouTube channels with in-depth tutorials on machine learning.

No matter how you proceed now, keep this book handy because it will help you find answers quickly. One of the problems learning with online resources is that you will quickly forget where you saw something particular and waste a lot of time searching for it. In all honesty, bookmarks are still a thing that make books better.

Where Will Machine Learning Be in the Next 20 Years?

Machine learning is already penetrating every walk of life, and the trend will continue to grow unless there's a world-wide catastrophe that completely stops the internet. Since someone remarked, "Data is the new oil," industry experts have argued how valuable user data truly is for businesses and why there's a need to give everyone the ability to monetize access to their data.

The social media platform you joined for free just to connect with your friends years ago now shows you targeted ads, which the advertisement company is heavily charged, and on top of that, sells your data to data aggregators. Do you think the transaction is fair?

There is definitely a need to monitor and control what data companies can access and for what reason. The European (General Data Protection Regulation) GDPR is a very good initiative in this regard. I hope more countries follow suit and adapt GDPR to their local internet industry. Too much good stuff is also bad for you!

But, the future is not gloom and doom. Machine learning is already making lives easier and as more industries become aware of its capabilities, it will become easier to gradually optimize their services. Consider a fully capable artificially intelligent robot providing medical services in places where there's an extreme shortage of doctors and health facilities. Imagine a house that's aware of your needs and correspondingly prepares everyday like clockwork without any manual adjustments. The future feels good!

References

Cortez, P. and Silva A. *Using Data Mining to Predict Secondary School Student Performance*. In A. Brito and J. Teixeira Eds., Proceedings of 5th FUture BUsiness TEChnology Conference (FUBUTEC 2008) pp. 5-12, Porto, Portugal, April, 2008, EUROSIS, ISBN 978-9077381-39-7

Geron, Aurelien. *Hands-On Machine Learning with Scikit-Learn & TensorFlow*. 2d. ed. 1005 Gravenstein Highway North, Sebastopol, CA 95472: O'Reilly Publication, 2016

Rashka, Sebastian. *Python Machine Learning*. 1st. ed. 35 Livery Street, Birmingham B3 2PB, UK: Packt Publishing Ltd., 2015

Appendix A: Machine-Learning Concepts

This will be a brief chapter where we will explore the theoretical background of various machine-learning concepts that you will encounter from time to time.

Data Scrubbing

A process that runs in the background to fix errors in the main memory through periodical inspections is called data scrubbing. The errors are fixed with redundant data, such as duplicating existing data or using checksums. Data scrubbing removes varied and unique error instances with the same error that makes it easier to filter and fix.

In data analytics and machine learning, we know that data integrity is vital to get correct results from the implementation of an algorithm. Whenever data is accessed from an unreliable source, it should first be error-checked before any action is performed on it. Data is inherently dirty (having errors) and has a tendency of fallback to dirtiness even after cleaning. Incorrect data can lead to wrong decisions that in turn can cause huge business losses. Most companies that utilize data analysis and machine learning in Customer Relationship Management (CRM), marketing tools and Business Intelligence (BI) software cite dealing with inconsistent data as the biggest issue. It's like putting low-grade gas in your car. It might sound better due to cheaper rates and no immediate signs of significant decrease in performance. But, in the long run, it's going to ruin the car's engine.

The quality of data used for analysis and predictions is the difference between successful and failing businesses.

But, how you would error check without knowing if some data is correct or not? You have to find inconsistencies in data or check for the possibility of missing data. All computer systems have some sort of error checking so these errors don't affect the output. Data analysts and scientists have to take care of data scrubbing themselves.

The future belongs to the Internet of Things (IoT) where all the systems will be connected to provide seamless functionality. Every system produces a mammoth amount of data and joining them together to create a supersystem would mean every subsystem should be able to understand data generated by another subsystem. Standardizing data production and transmission will be necessary along with implementation of highly precise data scrubbing methods.

In the long term, data scrubbing helps in determining the cause of errors that must be fixed in order for the system to improve its performance. Even after the errors are removed, data scrubbing must not be removed from the system. Using machine learning with data scrubbing results in a self-learning completely automatic error detection and correction system that can even predict when an error will occur by analyzing system parameters.

For example, you have written a code that continuously downloads data from a statistical website. The data scrubbing module actively checks the data to ensure there's no missing or erroneous data. The internet connection goes down that leads to missing data (nulls and NaNs) being fed to the system. The data scrubbing module checks for possible reasons and learns that it's due to a faulty internet connection. Now, whenever our script will start getting missing data, the data scrubbing module will check the internet connection. If it's down, it will try to reconnect, and if that fails, it will pause data import and notify the user through available methods of the problem. This way, the data scrubbing module will keep self-learning whenever a new error is met. Lastly, here's a data scrubbing checklist for quick reference.

- Identify frequent sources of error and create a pattern. The sources can be anything from bad internet connection to incorrect data import settings.
- Check for all common data issues such as finding duplicates and missing data. Investigate data with respect to the data standardization rules to identify inconsistencies.
- Clean the data from all errors and inconsistencies.
- Update the data and system regularly, so they are always working with the latest tools and standards.
- Secure access to the data and the system by deploying stringent data security processes including staff training.

- <u>Comply</u> with all the regulatory laws and regulations governing the data. An example is full compliance with GDPR for your website data.
- <u>Enrich</u> user experience by using high quality data that allows for better user insights.

Neural Network

A set of algorithms created to mimic the working of a human mind is called neural networks. Humans deduce outcomes using patterns and neural networks also aim to use the same technique to reach conclusions.

Neural networks are chiefly used in classification and clustering. Neural networks can be combined with other machine learning algorithms to predict behavior of complex systems. Neural networks are made of numerous layers, each can have different properties (arguments). Each layer in itself is made from nodes, which are called neurons. The layers act as input and output of the neural network. The neurons act as binary diodes that either switch on or off in response to an input.

The layer structure helps neural networks to find relationship between data attributes that isn't possible with other single-layer predictive algorithms. The input data goes through each layer just like a car goes through an automated car washing facility.

Neural networks form the basis of deep learning because generally neural network algorithms deploy three or more layers. The input of each layer is the output of the previous layer (except the first layer that takes the raw data). Many machine-learning experts consider neural networks as makeshift AI because the layers act in a sequence on the data to reach a conclusion. Neural networks are great at predicting the working of a complex system but fail to establish the actual relationship between the input and the output.

Decision Trees

Decision trees contain a series of nodes much like a flowchart that the user can use to predict the probability of an event by following the node path. Decision trees are easier to understand for non-technical personnel. They are not greatly affected by missing data or outliers, which means less time and resources are needed to clean the data. There are some disadvantages as well. One of the biggest disadvantages of using decision trees is overfitting.

Decision trees are better for systems that have non-linear relationships between its attributes. The algorithms mostly rely on supervised machine learning. Each internal node acts corresponds to a system attribute and each leaf (external) node corresponds to a classification label. Decision trees are also very similar nested sets of "if", "then", and "else" statements which makes them easier to code. There are two types of decision trees.

1. Continuous variable decision tree: a decision tree that has a continuous target variable (regression algorithms)

2. <u>Categorical variable decision tree:</u> a decision tree where the target variable has specific categories (classification algorithms)

If the system data has high variance (very frequent data changes in the data), decision trees might be difficult but not impossible to implement. Decision trees are the algorithm version of Julius Caesar's famous quote "divide and conquer." The "sklearn" library provides a module "tree" that can be used to create and work with decision trees in Python. Decision trees are inverse of natural trees in the perspective of location of roots and leaves. In a decision tree, the leaves (terminal nodes) lie at the bottom while roots are at the top. It also means a decision tree has a top-to-bottom hierarchy.

Algorithm Selection

You have read about and coded various predictive algorithms throughout this book. You might be wondering which algorithm is best at predicting a situation. The answer is, it depends on a lot of factors. There is no "one for all situations" algorithm. As a data scientist, it will be your responsibility to analyze the system data and behavior and choose the best model you think most closely represent a given system. You will have to find the relationship between system attributes, usually it's done by plotting a trend of different system attributes. Once, the relationship is estimated, the correct model is picked along with the algorithm ideal for the specific system attribute relationship.

It is important to understand that you can misinterpret the data and pick the wrong model, leading to an algorithm implementation that will not give accurate and precise predictions. A good data scientist will always keep this in mind and rigorously analyze the system attribute data from different perspectives before moving to pick a predictive algorithm. To automate this process, the data scientist might train different models using the data set and compare prediction results to choose one of them.

Data Mining

The process of inspecting large data sets and finding patterns by combining techniques of machine learning, database systems, and statistics is called data mining. It is very useful to detect patterns in data that might not be easily apparent. When we say data mining, we are actually not mining data, but mining what the data represents.

The process of data mining has usually six parts (these processes are not sequential).

1. Anomaly detection: The process of finding an outlier, deviation, spike, drop, or a huge change from the majority of data points that might be errors or interesting instances to investigate.
2. Dependency modeling: Also known as association rule learning, the purpose is to find relationship between different attributes of a system.

3. Clustering: The procedure of finding groups or clusters of similar data points in a system is called clustering without prior knowledge of data.
4. Classification: The process of labeling or generalizing new data according to preset data structure is called classification. We have already seen this in action in our book.
5. Regression: The process of finding a function model that fits the entirety or majority of the data set. This helps in dependency modeling.
6. Summarization: This process provides a concise data set representation through many methods including data visualization and report generation.

Data mining can be used wherever you can find digital data. This has led to several cases of data misuse. It is the responsibility of the data accumulators/aggregators to make sure the data collected is only available for the purposes the data is collected for. Implementation of stricter rules is a big problem, but the EU is way ahead of North America in this respect. Unfortunately, there will be no way to completely stop data misuse in the future no matter how strict rules are implemented. This is one of the biggest challenges in Internet of Things (IoT).

Printed in Poland
by Amazon Fulfillment
Poland Sp. z o.o., Wrocław